Warman's

W9-BXX-595

Depression Glass

FIELD GUIDE

3rd Edition

Ellen T. Schroy

Values and Identification

©2008 Krause Publications

Published by

 krause publications

An Imprint of F+W Publications

700 East State Street • Iola, WI 54990-0001
715-445-2214 • 888-457-2873
www.krausebooks.com

Our toll-free number to place an order or obtain
a free catalog is (800) 258-0929.

Library of Congress Control Number: 2007940677

ISBN-13: 978-0-89689-621-5

ISBN-10: 0-89689-621-8

Designed by Donna Mummery

Edited by Dan Brownell

Printed in China

Many hom
I could not have created this book.

Thumbnails of Depression Glass Patterns

Jerry O'Brien

Photography

Donna Chiarelli
Rick Hirte
Fran Jay
Mildred McCurdy
Neil McCurdy
Al and Rubie Myers
Troy Vozzella
James Hintz
Tina Trautman
Ron and Julie Madlung

CONTENTS

Color Swatches

Due to variations within batches, patterns, and thicknesses, glass colors are
a bit subjective. We have done our best to represent what is available. We do
hope the color swatches will aid readers in identifying items.

INTRODUCTION

The wonderful colored glassware that collectors love to call "Depression glass" actually would be called something different if glass-researcher Hazel Marie Weatherman had her way. She referred to it as "rainbow glass" because of the beautiful colors. She also tried calling it "candy glass" but the name that really has stuck since the first collectors started to buy it is "Depression glass." This term refers to those dark days in America's past when money was tight, but the country was also on the cusp of an industrial revolution. That revolution took some of the hard labor of creating handmade glassware from detailed patterned glass molds into a new industry as glass making machines were being developed that would allow the manufacturers to make more and more glass at reasonable prices. Today's collectors are very mindful of that when they are out searching for Depression glass at flea markets, yard sales, and even antique shows. They know if they keep searching, they have a very good chance of finding that perfect piece.

The Depression glass collector of this century has it a little easier than the original collectors did. We have the benefit of the Internet, where we can look up patterns, research any known reproductions, find dealers easily, and even buy glassware with a few clicks on our keyboard. Assuming that most patterns were bought new from the 1920s up to the 1950s, you then must allow a little time for folks to use them, perhaps break a few pieces, and then get relegated to the back of the cupboard and languish there until a new family member pulls it out and becomes excited over the find. Ideally, the new owner will then decide to try to find out what pattern it is, who made it, if are there more pieces, and then start to research how to find those pieces. Sometimes the new collector will be satisfied using modern reproductions to fill in the gaps, perhaps intending to only use the reproductions until they can find vintage pieces. Happily for collectors, the repro makers are losing interest in making Depression glass patterns that are meant to deceive the buyer. Some newer Depression-era looking patterns are turning up, but in colors never available before. These patterns serve the same purpose the original 1920s to 1950s glassware did—they allow the owners to set a very pretty table, often inexpensively, and give a nice change to china services. Look for the † marking in this edition to alert you to known reproductions. Also become familiar with what colors the pattern was originally made in to avoid becoming confused if other colors start appearing at yard sales and flea markets.

Finding a Depression-era pattern that appeals to you can be an exciting adventure. Learning about who made it, when, what kind of colors were created, and what forms you like best is part of what makes collecting so much fun. Today many collector clubs specialize in researching glassware as well as offering online discussion groups. Becoming involved in these kinds of groups will definitely enhance the joy of collecting. Consider visiting the

West Virginia Museum of American Glass, Main Avenue, PO Box 574, Weston, WV 26452, or better yet, become a member so you can get a subscription to their excellent quarterly publication, *All About Glass.* This magazine covers all periods of glassware, and often features very interesting articles as well as reprints of vintage ads that help define Depression glass and how it was manufactured, as it explores other interests of the glass collecting world. Knowledge is the key for any collector, and being armed with a good reference book, like this edition of *Warman's Depression Glass,* will certainly give any collector an edge to fulfilling their dream of cupboards filled with rainbows of sparkling colored glass.

Bubble, sapphire blue grill plate, platter, soup bowl, and 4" d berry bowl.

Princess, green candy jar.

19th C Ohio Flint Glass founded, later becomes part of National Glass Company conglomerate.
Indiana Glass Company established in 1907.
Bottle plant at Jeannette, Pennsylvania, which becomes Jeannette Glass Company.

1853 McKee and Brothers founded in Pittsburgh, Pennsylvania.

1887 Fostoria Glass Company, founded in Fostoria, Ohio, but moves to Moundsville, West Virginia, when fuel supply is depleted.

1888 McKee moves to Jeannette, Pennsylvania.

1890 Westmoreland Specialty Company established in Grapeville, Pennsylvania. Early manufacture includes bottles and food containers. During World War I, glass candy containers are made. The plant continues on to make colored and opaque glassware in both Depression patterns and later a giftware line.

1891 U.S. Glass Company organizes by combining 18 different glass houses located in Pennsylvania, Ohio, and West Virginia. The main offices, as well as some manufacturing, are in Pittsburgh.

1899   Macbeth merges with Evans, creating Macbeth-Evans. Main factory located in Charleroi, Pennsylvania, with others located in Marion, Bethevan, and Elwood, Indiana, as well as Toledo, Ohio.

1900   Federal Glass Company opens Columbus, Ohio, plant. First wares are crystal with needle etching, various decorations, and crackle finish. After switching to automation, they soon begin production of tumblers and many Depression-era patterns, as well as restaurant wares, all at an economical price.

1901   Imperial Glass Company organizes. Produces first glass at Bellaire, Ohio, plant in 1904.
Morgantown Glass Works begins production in Morgantown, West Virginia.
New Martinsville Glass Manufacturing Company is established at New Martinsville, West Virginia.

1902   Hazel Atlas Glass Company established in Washington, Pennsylvania, a result of the merger of the Hazel Glass Company and its neighboring factory, Atlas Glass and Metal Company. Corporate offices are later established at Wheeling, West Virginia.

1903   Morgantown Glass Works reorganizes as Economy Tumbler Company and operates using that name.

Liberty Cut Glass Works established in Egg Harbor, New Jersey. Primarily a cutting house for years, pressed glass is also made.

McKee Brothers reorganizes into McKee Glass Company and continues until 1951.

1905   Anchor Hocking Glass Company established in Lancaster, Ohio. Well known by the mid-1920s for their tumbler and tableware production.

1906   Fenton Art Glass Company builds new factory in Williamstown, West Virginia. While their giftware lines are well known, some Depression-era glassware is produced.

1907   Indiana Glass Company established at Dunkirk, Indiana. Early production is hand pressed. Assembly line patterns evolve during the 1920s, although some still require hand work. Later produces automobile glassware items and becomes a subsidiary of Lancaster Colony.

1908   Lancaster Glass Company, Lancaster, Ohio, built by first president of Fostoria.

1911   L.E. Smith begins in the glass trade. A lot of the production of this company remains utilitarian in nature as well as making lenses for automobiles.

1916   Paden City Glass Manufacturing Company established
at Paden City, West Virginia. Production includes some
Depression-era patterns, but more well known for elegant
lines, vases, lamps, and restaurant wares.

1923   Economy Tumbler Company changes name to Economy
Glass Company.

1924   Fostoria introduces color and starts national magazine
advertising campaign.
Jeannette touted by trade as "one of the most complete
automatic factories in the country."
Lancaster becomes subsidiary of Hocking Glass Company.
Continues to make kitchenware, cut and decorative
tableware under the Lancaster name until 1937. Also
makes colored blanks for Standard Glass Company, another
Hocking subsidiary, where the glass is etched and cut.
Known as Plant #2 to Anchor Hocking.

1927   Jeannette management ceases all hand operations.

1928   Jeannette makes green and pink glass automatically in a
continuous tank, a first!
Trade journals proclaim Clarksburg, West Virginia, Hazel-
Atlas factory the "World's Largest Tumbler Factory," which
accurately describes the fully automated factory.

Cloverleaf, green saucer, pink plate, and pink cup.

1929 Economy Glass Company changes name back to Morgantown Glass Works, Inc.

1932 Liberty Cut Glass Works destroyed by fire, never to rebuild.

1937 Corning Glass Works purchases Macbeth-Evans.
Hocking Glass Company merges with Anchor Cap and Closure Corporation, Long Island City, New York, creating the huge Anchor-Hocking Glass Company, which has continued to have a major impact on the glassware industry.
Morgantown Glass Works, Inc., closes.

1938 U.S. Glass moves main offices to Tiffin, Ohio, and production decreases.

1939 Morgantown Glassware Guild organizes and reopens factory.

1944 New Martinsville sold and reorganizes as Viking Glass Company.

1949 Westmoreland Glass Company begins to use impressed intertwined "W" and "G" mark.

1951 The only operating company of the former U.S. Glass is Tiffin. The rest have all closed.
McKee sold to Thatcher Manufacturing Co.

1952   Fire destroys Belmont plant, Bellaire, Ohio, and with the fire go company records.

1955   Duncan and Miller molds acquired by Tiffin, which begins to produce colors and crystal wares with these molds.

1956   Continental Can purchases Hazel-Atlas and continues to sell tableware under the name "Hazelware."

1958   Federal Glass becomes a division of Federal Paper Board Company, and continues glassware production.

1961   Jeannette buys old McKee factory in Jeannette and moves there to continue production.

1964   Brockway Glass Company buys out Continental Can's interest in Hazel-Atlas and begins operation.

1965   Fostoria Glass Company purchases Morgantown Glassware Guild.

1966   Continental Can takes over operation of Tiffin until 1969, with glass production continuing.

1971   Glass production terminated at Fostoria's Morgantown facility, ending the Morgantown Glassware Guild.

1973   Imperial Glass Company sold to Lenox, Inc.

1980   Tiffin Glass discontinues operation.

1982   Westmoreland Glass Company closes factory in May. Reorganizes in July.

1983   Lancaster Glass purchases Fostoria. Westmoreland begins to use full name as imprinted mark.

1984   Westmoreland Glass Company again closes Grapeville plant.

1999   L.G. Wright discontinues operation. Molds, factory equipment liquidated at public auction in May.

2000   Indiana Glass goes out of business in November.

2004   L.E. Smith ceases production in June.

2007   Fenton announces plans to close factory.

Cracked Ice, pink creamer and covered sugar.

COLOR TIMELINE

AMBER

1923: McKee

1923: New Martinsville

1924: Paden City

1924: Westmoreland's Transparent Amber

1924-1941: Fostoria

1925: Indiana

Mid-1920s: Hocking, Imperial and L.E. Smith

1926: Jeannette

Late 1920s: Liberty

1931-1942: Federal's Golden Glow

1960: Westmoreland's Golden Sunset

AMETHYST

1923: McKee

1924: New Martinsville

Mid-1920s: L.E. Smith

1926: Morgantown's Old Amethyst

1933: Paden City

1939: Morgantown's Light Amethyst

APPLE GREEN

1925: Jeannette

BLACK

1920s-1930s: L.E. Smith

1922: Morgantown's India Black

1923 and 1930s: Paden City

1923: New Martinsville

1924: Fostoria

1930: McKee

1931: Hazel-Atlas, Imperial, Lancaster

BLUE

1920s: Lancaster

1923: McKee's Jap Blue and Transparent Blue

1923: New Martinsville

1924: Paden City

1924-1928: Fostoria

Cherry Blossom, 4-3/4" d. Delphite bowls.

1925: McKee's Sky Blue and Westmoreland's

Mid-1920s: Hocking

1926: Imperial, Morgantown's Azure and transparent blue

1927: Imperial's Blue-Green, Morgantown's Ritz

1928: New Martinsville's Alice Blue (medium shade)

1928-1943: Fostoria's Azure Blue (lighter shade)

Late 1920s: Liberty's pale shade

1930: Hocking's Mayfair Blue (medium shade), McKee's Ritz Blue and Chalaine Blue

1931: Imperial's Ritz Blue, Lancaster's pale blue, Westmoreland's Belgian Blue

1933: Fostoria's Regal Blue

1933-1934: Federal's Madonna Blue (medium shade)

1933-1942: New Martinsville's Ritz Blue

Mid 1930s: MacBeth-Evans' Ritz Blue

1936: Hazel-Atlas's Ritz Blue, McKee's opaque Poudre Blue, Paden City's Ceylon Blue

1939: Morgantown's Copen Blue and Gloria Blue

1940: Anchor-Hocking's Fire King

1950s: Indiana's Blue-Green

BURGUNDY

1933: Fostoria

1936: Hazel-Atlas (deep shade)

CANARY YELLOW

1923: McKee

Mid-1920s: Hocking, L.E. Smith

1924: New Martinsville

1924-1927: Fostoria

1925: Lancaster

COBALT BLUE

1930: Liberty

1936: Paden City

1939: Morgantown

CREMAX

1939: MacBeth-Evans

CRYSTAL

1923: Paden City

1930s: Imperial

1935: New Martinsville and Westmoreland—most companies produced crystal throughout their years of production

DELPHITE, DELFITE

1936: Jeannette

FIRED-ON COLORS

1920s: Federal and Lancaster

1923: Westmoreland

1926: New Martinsville

Mid-1930s: MacBeth-Evans

FRENCH IVORY (OPAQUE)

1933: McKee

GREEN

1920s: Lancaster

1921: Morgantown's Venetian Green

1922: Morgantown's Meadow Green

1923: McKee

1924: Paden City

1924-1941: Fostoria

Mid-1920s: Hocking, Imperial and L.E. Smith

1925: Indiana, McKee's Grass Green and New Martinsville

1926: New Martinsville's Emerald Green

1926-1936: Federal's Springtime Green

1928: MacBeth-Evans' Emerald

Late 1920s: Liberty

1929: Hazel-Atlas, Imperial

1931: Morgantown's Stiegel Green

1931-1933: New Martinsville's Stiegel Green

1933: Fostoria's Empire Green, Hazel-Atlas's Killarney Green, New Martinsville's Evergreen (dark shade)

1936: Paden City's Forest Green

1939: Morgantown's Shamrock Green

1950s: Anchor-Hocking's Forest Green

IRIDESCENT

1920s: Federal

1920s to present: Jeannette

1934-1935: Federal's Iridescent Amber

IVORY

1929: Imperial

1933: Indiana (opaque)

1940: Anchor-Hocking

IVRENE

1930s: MacBeth-Evans

JADE

1930: McKee

1931: New Martinsville

JADE YELLOW

1923: McKee

JADITE

1932: Jeannette

MONAX

1920s: MacBeth-Evans

MULBERRY

1924: Paden City

OPALESCENT

1923: Morgantown's Alabaster

Anniversary iridescent dinner plate.

1931: Westmoreland's Moonstone (blue)

1942: Anchor-Hocking's Moonstone

ORCHID

1927: McKee

1927-1929: Fostoria

1929: Imperial

PINK

Mid-1920s: Imperial's Rose Marie, Rose

1925: Paden City's Cheriglo

1926: McKee's Rose Pink, Morgantown's Anna

RED-AMBER

1930: Liberty

ROSE

1926: Indiana and Westmoreland

1926-1942: Hocking's Rose (later called Flamingo or Cerise), New Martinsville's Peach Melba (later known as Rose)

1927: Jeannette's Wild Rose, L.E. Smith

1928: MacBeth-Evans

1928-1941: Fostoria's Rose or Dawn

Late 1920s: Liberty

1930: Hazel-Atlas, Lancaster's deep pink

1931-1942: Federal's Rose Glow

1933: Hazel-Atlas's Sunset Pink

1939: Morgantown's Pink Champagne

1947-1949: Jeannette

ROYAL BLUE

1932: Paden City

RUBY

1925: Morgantown

1927: McKee

1931: Imperial

1932: Paden City

1933-1942: New Martinsville

Mid-1930s: MacBeth-Evans

1935: Fostoria's Ruby

1939: Anchor-Hocking's Royal Ruby

SEA FOAM

1931: Imperial, Harding Blue, Moss Green, or Burnt Almond with opal edge

SEVILLE YELLOW

1931: McKee

SHELL PINK

1958: Jeannette

SKOKIE GREEN

1931: McKee

TAN

1931: McKee's Old Rose

TOPAZ

1921: Morgantown's 14K Topaz

1925: Jeannette

1928: Hocking

1929: Fostoria

1930: Lancaster, Westmoreland (sometimes combined with crystal or black)

Mid-1930s: Indiana

1931: Imperial, Liberty, MacBeth-Evans, McKee, Paden City's Golden Glow

1933: Hazel-Atlas

1938-1940s: Fostoria's Golden Tint

1939: Morgantown's Topaz Mist

ULTRAMARINE

1937-1938: Jeannette

Beaded Block, vaseline square plate, and iridescent round plate.

VASELINE

Mid-1920s: Imperial

WHITE

1930s: Hazel-Atlas's Platonite (opaque)

1932: Hocking (Vitrock)

1937-1942: McKee (opal) and after World War II

WINE

1923: New Martinsville

WISTERIA

1931-1938: Fostoria

Vitrock, white salad plate and cereal bowl.

THUMBNAIL GUIDE

For more listings, photos, and thumbnails, consult *Warman's Depression Glass, 4th edition,* which can be purchased at your local bookstore, or directly from the publisher online at www.krausebooks.com, or by phone at (800) 258-0929.

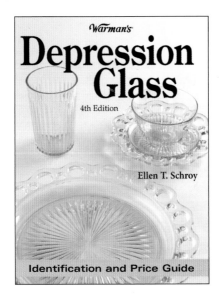

ART DECO	BASKETS

Ovide
(see page 324)

Lorain
(see page 263)

BIRDS

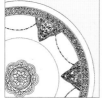

Georgian
(see page 222)

Parrot
(see page 332)

BLOCKS

Beaded Block
(see page 71)

Colonial Block
(see page 124)

BOWS	CUBES

Bowknot
(see page 82)

Cube
(see page 137)

DIAMONDS

Diamond Quilted
(see page 155)

English Hobnail
(see page 176)

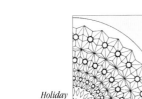

Holiday
(see page 234)

Laced Edge
(see page 253)

DIAMONDS

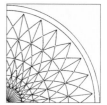

Miss America
(see page 286)

Waterford
(see page 457)

Windsor
(see page 464)

ELLIPSES

Newport
(see page 310)

FLORALS

Cherry Blossom
(see page 101)

Cloverleaf
(see page 115)

FLORALS

Daisy
(see page 144)

Dogwood
(see page 164)

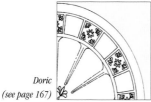

Doric
(see page 167)

Doric & Pansy
(see page 169)

Floragold
(see page 194)

Floral
(see page 197)

FLORALS

Floral &
Diamond Band
(see page 207)

Flower Garden with
Butterflies
(see page 211)

Indiana Custard
(see page 244)

Iris
(see page 246)

Jubilee
(see page 250)

Mayfair
(Federal)
(see page 275)

FLORALS

Mayfair
(Open Rose)
(see page 277)

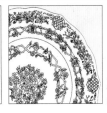

Normandie
(see page 313)

Pineapple & Floral
(see page 344)

Rosemary
(see page 375)

Rose Cameo
(see page 373)

Royal Lace
(see page 384)

FLORALS

Sharon
(see page 409)

Sunflower
(see page 429)

Thistle
(see page 437)

Tulip
(see page 441)

Vitrock
(see page 455)

FIGURES

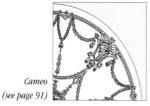

Cameo
(see page 91)

Cupid
(see page 141)

FRUITS

Avocado
(see page 68)

Cherryberry
(see page 106)

Della Robbia
(see page 148)

Fruits
(see page 220)

Strawberry
(see page 424)

GEOMETRIC & LINE DESIGNS

Cracked Ice
(see page 133)

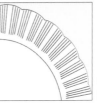

Cremax
(see page 135)

Early American Prescut
(see page 172)

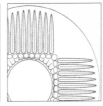

Park Avenue
(see page 330)

Pioneer
(see page 347)

Sierra
(see page 415)

GEOMETRIC & LINE DESIGNS

Star
(see page 419)

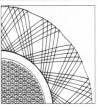

Starlight
(see page 421)

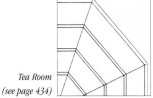

Tea Room
(see page 434)

Wexford
(see page 460)

HONEYCOMB

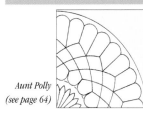

Aunt Polly
(see page 64)

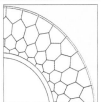

Hex Optic
(see page 229)

HORSESHOE	INDENTED CIRCLES	LACY DESIGNS

Horseshoe
(see page 241)

Capri
(see page 96)

Harp
(see page 225)

LACY DESIGNS

Heritage
(see page 227)

S-Pattern
(see page 393)

Sandwich (Duncan & Miller) *Sandwich (Hocking)*
(see page 397) *(see page 402)*

Sandwich (Indiana)
(see page 406)

LEAVES

Laurel
(see page 257)

Sunburst
(see page 427)

LOOPS

Christmas Candy
(see page 110)

Old Colony
(see page 319)

Pretzel
(see page 349)

PETALS

Aurora
(see page 66)

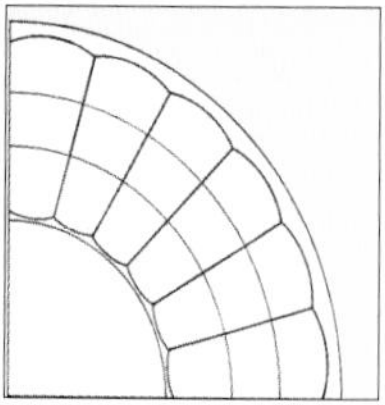

Block Optic
(see page 77)

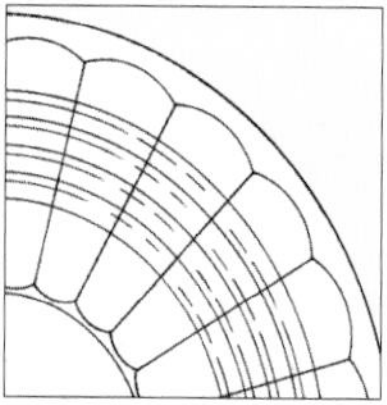

Circle
(see page 112)

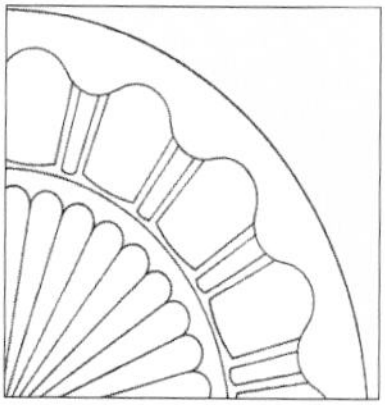

Colonial
(see page 118)

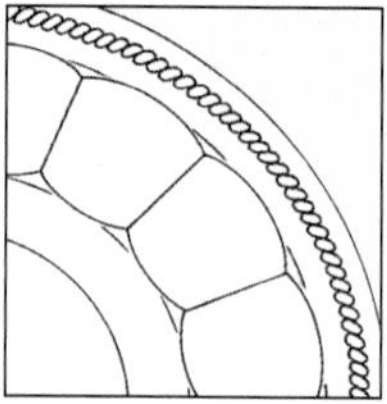

Colonial Fluted
(see page 126)

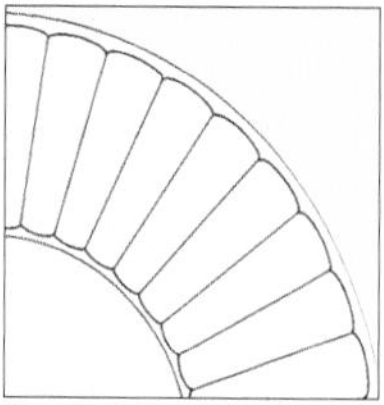

National
(see page 304)

PETALS

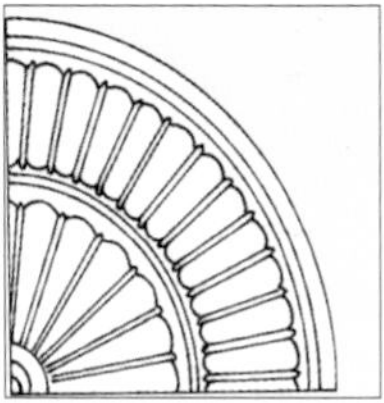

New Century
(see page 307)

Old Café
(see page 315)

Ribbon
(see page 367)

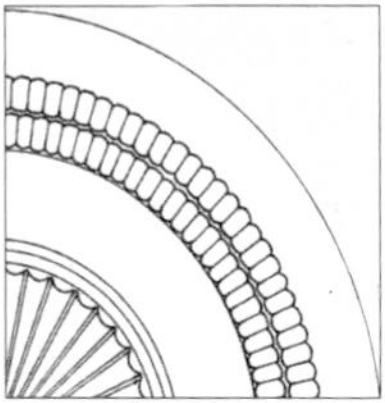

Roulette
(see page 377)

Round Robin
(see page 380)

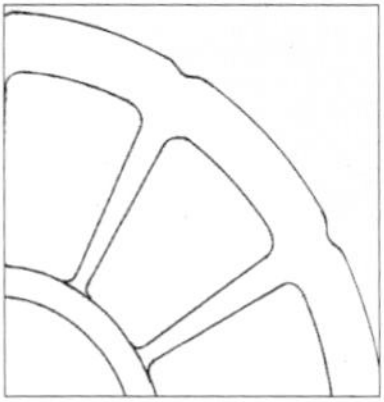

Victory
(see page 452)

PETALS OR RIDGES WITH DIAMOND ACCENTS

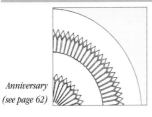

Anniversary
(see page 62)

Coronation
(see page 131)

Fortune
(see page 218)

Lincoln Inn
(see page 260)

Petalware
(see page 340)

Queen Mary
(see page 360)

Thumbnail Guide

PLAIN	PYRAMIDS

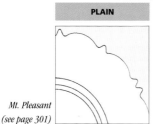

Mt. Pleasant
(see page 301)

Pyramid
(see page 358)

RAISED BAND

Forest Green
(see page 214)

Royal Ruby
(see page 387)

RAISED CIRCLES

American Pioneer
(see page 54)

Bubble
(see page 84)

RAISED CIRCLES

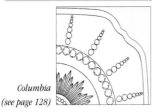

Columbia
(see page 128)

Dewdrop
(see page 152)

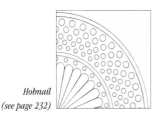

Hobnail
(see page 232)

Moonstone
(see page 295)

Oyster & Pearls
(see page 327)

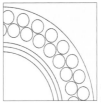

Raindrops
(see page 364)

RAISED CIRCLES

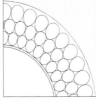

Ships
(see page 412)

Thumbprint
(see page 439)

RIBS

Homespun
(see page 238)

RINGS (CIRCLES)

Manhattan
(see page 271)

Moondrops
(see page 290)

RINGS (CIRCLES)

Moroccan Amethyst
(see page 298)

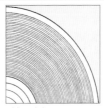

Old English
(see page 322)

Ring
(see page 369)

SCENES

Chinex Classic
(see page 108)

Lake Como
(see page 255)

SCROLLING DESIGNS

Adam
(see page 50)

American
Sweetheart
(see page 57)

SCROLLING DESIGNS

Florentine No.1
(see page 203)

Florentine No.2
(see page 206)

Madrid
(see page 266)

Patrick
(see page 338)

Primo
(see page 352)

Princess
(see page 354)

SCROLLING DESIGNS

Roxana
(see page 382)

Vernon
(see page 450)

SWIRLS

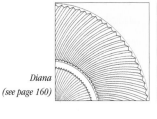

Diana
(see page 160)

Fairfax
(see page 187)

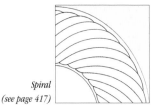

Spiral
(see page 417)

Swirl
(see page 431)

SWIRLS

Twisted Optic
(see page 446)

U.S. Swirl
(see page 448)

TEXTURED

By Cracky
(see page 87)

Twiggy
(see page 443)

ADAM

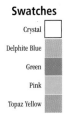

Swatches

Crystal

Delphite Blue

Green

Pink

Topaz Yellow

Manufactured by Jeannette Glass Company, Jeannette, Pa., from 1932 to 1934.

Made in crystal, Delphite blue, green, pink, some topaz and yellow. Delphite 4" h candlesticks are valued at $250 a pair. A yellow cup and saucer are valued at $200, and a 7-3/4" d yellow plate is valued at $115. Production in topaz and yellow was very limited. Crystal prices are approximately 50 percent of the prices listed for green.

Reproductions: † Butter dish in pink and green.

Item	Green	Pink
Ashtray, 4-1/2" d	$28	$30
Berry bowl, small	22.50	18.50
Bowl, 9" d, cov	90	75
Bowl, 9" d, open	45	30
Bowl, 10" l, oval	40	40

Item	Green	Pink
Butter dish, cov †	395	135
Cake plate, 10" d, ftd	38	40
Candlesticks, pr, 4" h	125	100
Candy jar, cov, 2-1/2" h	120	135
Casserole, cov	95	80
Cereal bowl, 5-3/4" d	50	40
Coaster, 3-1/4" d	32	35
Creamer	30	35
Cup	30	28
Dessert bowl, 4-3/4" d	25	25
Iced tea tumbler, 5-1/2" h	72	75

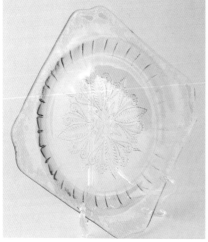

Adam, green salad plate $18.50.

Item	Green	Pink
Lamp	500	500
Pitcher, 32 oz, round base	-	125
Pitcher, 32 oz, 8" h	48	45
Plate, 6" d, sherbet	15	18
Plate, 7-3/4" d, salad, sq	18.50	19.50
Plate, 9" d, dinner, sq	37.50	42
Plate, 9" d, grill	37.50	35
Platter, 11-3/4" l, rect	38	38
Relish dish, 8" l, divided	27	20
Salt and pepper shakers, pr, 4" h	130	95
Sherbet, 3"	40	38
Sugar, cov	48	65
Tumbler, 4-1/2" h	35	40
Vase, 7-1/2" h	60	550
Vegetable bowl, 7-3/4" d	30	40

Adam, green ashtray $28, and pink pitcher $45.

Adam, 10" pink oval bowl $40.

Adam, pink covered butter $135.

AMERICAN PIONEER

Swatches

Amber
Crystal
Green
Pink

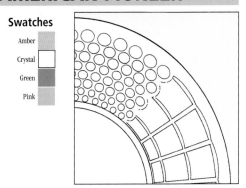

Manufactured by Liberty Works, Egg Harbor, N.J., from 1931 to 1934. Made in amber, crystal, green, and pink.

Item	Amber	Crystal	Green	Pink
Bowl, 5" d, handle	$45	$24	$27.50	$24
Bowl, 8-3/4" d, cov	-	115	125	115
Bowl, 9" d, handle	-	24	30	24
Bowl, 9-1/4" d, cov	-	120	150	120
Bowl, 10" d	-	50	70	60
Candlesticks, pr, 6-1/2" h	-	75	95	75
Candy jar, cov, 1 pound	-	100	115	110
Candy jar, cov, 1-1/2 pound	-	70	125	95
Cheese and cracker set, indented plate and compote	-	50	65	55

Item	Amber	Crystal	Green	Pink
Coaster, 3-1/2" d	-	30	35	32
Cocktail, 3 oz, 3-13/16" h	45	-	-	-
Cocktail, 3-1/2 oz, 3 -15/16" h	45	-	-	-
Console bowl, 10-3/4" d	-	50	75	60
Creamer, 2-3/4" h	-	20	22	25
Creamer, 3-1/2" h	60	30	32	30
Cup	24	10	12	12
Dresser set, 2 cologne bottles, powder jar, 7-1/2" tray	-	300	345	365
Goblet, 8 oz, 6" h, water	-	40	45	40
Ice bucket, 6" h	-	90	95	95
Juice tumbler, 5 oz	-	40	45	40
Lamp, 1-3/4", metal pole, 9-1/2"	-	-	85	-
Lamp, 5-1/2" round, ball shape	175	-	-	70
Lamp, 8-1/2" h	-	90	115	110
Mayonnaise, 4-1/4"	-	75	115	95
Pilsner, 5-3/4" h, 11 oz	-	100	110	100
Pitcher, cov, 5" h	295	150	225	165
Pitcher, cov, 7" h	325	175	250	195
Plate, 6" d	-	12.50	17.50	12.50
Plate, 6" d, handle	25	12.50	17.50	12.50
Plate, 8" d	28	10	13	14
Plate, 11-1/2" d, handle	40	20	24	20
Rose bowl, 4-1/4" d, ftd	-	40	50	45
Saucer, 6" sq	10	4.50	5	5.50
Sherbet, 3-1/2" h	-	20	25	20
Sherbet, 4-3/4" h	65	32.50	40	30
Sugar, 2-3/4" h	-	20	27.50	25
Sugar, 3-1/2" h	50	20	27.50	25
Tumbler, 8 oz, 4" h	-	32	55	35

Item	Amber	Crystal	Green	Pink
Tumbler, 12 oz, 5" h	-	60	65	60
Vase, 7" h, 4 styles	-	115	145	125
Vase, 9" h, round	-	-	245	-
Whiskey, 2 oz., 2-1/4" h	-	50	100	50

American Pioneer, green plate $13, cup $12, and saucer $5.

AMERICAN SWEETHEART

Swatches

■	Blue
■	Cremax
■	Monax
■	Pink
■	Red

Manufactured by Macbeth-Evans Glass Company, Charleroi, Pa., from 1930 to 1936.

Made in blue, Monax, pink, and red. Limited production in Cremax and color-trimmed Monax.

Item	Blue	Cremax	Monax
Berry bowl, 3-1/4"d, flat	$-	$-	$-
Berry bowl, 9" d	-	140	85
Cereal bowl, 6" d	-	19.50	20
Chop plate, 11" d	-	-	26
Console bowl, 18" d	1,450	-	550
Cream soup, 4-1/2" d	-	-	135
Creamer, ftd	195	-	15
Cup	160	-	15
Lamp shade	-	450	995

Item	Blue	Cremax	Monax
Pitcher, 60 oz, 7-1/2" h	-	-	-
Pitcher, 80 oz, 8" h	-	-	-
Plate, 6" d, bread and butter	-	-	7.50
Plate, 8" d, salad	135	-	12
Plate, 9" d, luncheon	-	-	19.50
Plate, 9-3/4" d, dinner	-	-	25
Plate, 10-1/4" d, dinner	-	-	30
Platter, 13" l, oval	-	-	85
Salt and pepper shakers, pr, ftd	-	-	395
Salver plate, 12" d	275	-	30
Saucer	25	-	7
Serving plate, 15-1/2" d	450	-	250
Sherbet, 4-1/4" h, ftd	-	-	25
Soup bowl, flat, 9-1/2" d	-	-	95
Sugar lid	-	-	300
Sugar, open, ftd	195	-	15

American Sweetheart, Monax open sugar $15, and creamer $15.

Item	Blue	Cremax	Monax
Tidbit, 2 tiers	350	-	95
Tidbit, 3 tiers	750	-	275
Tumbler, 5 oz, 3-1/2" h	-	-	-
Tumbler, 9 oz, 4-1/4" h	-	-	-
Tumbler, 10 oz, 4-3/4" h	-	-	-
Vegetable bowl, 11"	-	-	90

American Sweetheart, Monax 10-1/4" dinner plate $30.

American Sweetheart, 11" pink vegetable bowl $85.

American Sweetheart, 3-3/4" pink sherbet $30.

Item	Monax w/ color trim	Pink	Red
Berry bowl, 3-1/4"d, flat	$-	$90	$-
Berry bowl, 9" d	200	75	-
Cereal bowl, 6" d	50	28	-
Console bowl, 18" d	-	-	1,200
Cream soup, 4-1/2" d	-	100	-
Creamer, ftd	110	20	175
Cup	100	20	95
Pitcher, 60 oz, 7-1/2" h	-	995	-
Pitcher, 80 oz, 8" h	-	795	-
Plate, 6" d, bread and butter	24	10	-
Plate, 8" d, salad	30	15	145
Plate, 9" d, luncheon	48	-	-
Plate, 9-3/4" d, dinner	90	45	-
Plate, 10-1/4" d, dinner	-	45	-
Platter, 13" l, oval	225	75	-
Salt and pepper shakers, pr, ftd	-	500	-
Salver plate, 12" d	-	30	200
Saucer	18	7.50	45
Serving plate, 15-1/2" d	-	-	350
Sherbet, 3-3/4" h, ftd	-	30	-
Sherbet, 4-1/4" h, ftd	110	25	-
Soup bowl, flat, 9-1/2" d	170	85	-
Sugar, open, ftd	110	15	175
Tidbit, 2 tiers	-	250	-
Tidbit, 3 tiers	-	-	600
Tumbler, 5 oz, 3-1/2" h	-	130	-
Tumbler, 9 oz, 4-1/4" h	-	95	-
Tumbler, 10 oz, 4-3/4" h	-	185	-
Vegetable bowl, 11"	-	85	-

ANNIVERSARY

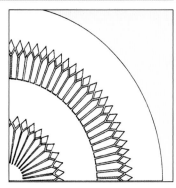

Swatches

Crystal

Iridescent

Pink

Manufactured by Jeannette Glass Company, Jeannette, Pa., from 1947 to 1949, and late 1960s to mid-1970s.

Made in crystal, iridescent, and pink.

Item	Crystal	Irid	Pink
Berry bowl, 4-7/8" d	$6.50	$5.50	$12
Butter dish, cov	25	-	50
Cake plate, 12-3/8" w, square	7	-	16.50
Cake plate, 12-1/2" d, round	18	-	18.50
Cake plate, metal cover	15	-	-
Candlesticks, pr, 4-7/8" h	20	25	-
Candy jar, cov	24	-	45
Compote, open, 3 legs	5	5	16
Compote, ruffled, 3 legs	6.50	-	-
Creamer, ftd	6	6.50	14
Cup	5	4	9

Item	Crystal	Irid	Pink
Fruit bowl, 9" d	15	14.50	24.50
Pickle dish 9" d	5.50	7.50	12
Plate, 9" d, dinner	8	8.50	18
Relish dish, 8" d	10	12.50	16
Saucer	1	1.50	6
Sherbet, ftd	10	-	12
Soup bowl, 7-3/8" d	8	7.50	18
Sugar, cov	12	10	20
Sugar, open, gold trim	4.50	-	-
Vase, 6-1/2" h	20	-	30
Wine, 2-1/2 oz	12	-	25

*Anniversary,
iridescent
dinner plate $8.50.*

AUNT POLLY

Swatches

Green

Blue

Iridescent

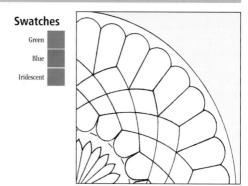

Manufactured by U.S. Glass Company, Pittsburgh, Pa., in the late 1920s.

Made in blue, green, and iridescent.

Item	Blue	Green	Irid
Berry bowl, 4-3/4" d, individual	$20	$15	$15
Berry bowl, 7-1/8" d, master	45	22	22
Bowl, 4-3/4" d, 2" h	-	15	15
Bowl, 5-1/2" d, one handle	25	15	15
Bowl, 8-3/8" l, oval	100	42	42
Butter dish, cov	225	210	200
Candy jar, cov, two handles	50	30	30
Candy jar, ftd, two handles	-	27.50	27.50
Creamer	60	32	32
Pickle, 7-1/4" l, oval, handle	45	20	20
Pitcher, 48 oz, 8" h	200	-	-

Item	Blue	Green	Irid
Plate, 6" d, sherbet	16	6	6
Plate, 8" d, luncheon	20	-	-
Salt and pepper shakers, pr	245	-	-
Sherbet	15	12	12
Sugar	195	95	95
Tumbler, 8 oz, 3-5/8" h	35	-	-
Vase, 6-1/2" h, ftd	55	35	38

*Aunt Polly,
blue sherbet
$15.*

AURORA

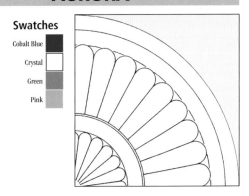

Swatches

Cobalt Blue

Crystal

Green

Pink

Manufactured by Hazel Atlas Glass Company, Clarksburg, W.V., and Zanesville, Ohio, in the late 1930s.

Made in cobalt (Ritz) blue, crystal, green, and pink.

Item	Cobalt Blue	Crystal	Green	Pink
Bowl, 4-1/2" d	$85	$-	$-	$75
Breakfast set, 24 pcs, service for 4	500	-	-	-
Cereal bowl, 5-3/8" d	20	12	9.50	15
Cup	20	6	10	15
Milk pitcher	27.50	-	-	25
Plate, 6-1/2" d	12.50	-	-	12.50
Saucer	7.50	2	3	6
Tumbler, 10 oz, 4-3/4" h	32.50	-	-	35.50

*Aurora, 4-1/2"d blue bowl (deep) $85,
5-3/8"d cereal bowl $20, and milk pitcher $27.50.*

AVOCADO

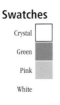

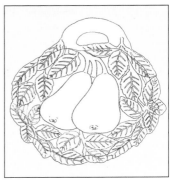

Manufactured by Indiana Glass Company, Dunkirk, Ind., from 1923 to 1933.

Made in crystal, green, pink, and white.

Reproductions: † Creamer, 8" pickle, 64 oz. pitcher, plates, sherbet, sugar, and tumblers. Reproductions can be found in amethyst, blue, dark green, frosted green, frosted pink, pink, red, and yellow, representing several colors not made originally.

Item	Crystal	Green	Pink	White
Bowl, 5-1/4" d, two handles	$12	$42	$45	$-
Bowl, 8" d, two handles, oval	17.50	35	30	-
Bowl, 8-1/2" d	20	60	50	-
Bowl, 9-1/2" d, 3-1/4" deep	25	175	150	-
Cake plate, 10-1/4" d, two handles	17.50	70	40	-
Creamer, ftd †	17.50	50	45	-

Item	Crystal	Green	Pink	White
Cup, ftd	-	40	45	-
Pickle bowl, 8" d, two handles, oval †	17.50	30	25	-
Pitcher, 64 oz †	385	950	900	425
Plate, 6-3/8" d, sherbet †	6	24	22	-
Plate, 8-1/4" d, luncheon †	7.50	27	20	-
Preserve bowl, 7" l, handle	10	32	28	-
Relish, 6" d, ftd	10	38	28	-
Salad bowl, 7-1/2" d	18	80	55.50	-
Saucer	6	24	15	-
Sherbet, ftd †	-	75	65	-
Sugar, ftd †	17.50	40	45	-
Tumbler †	25	250	150	35

Avocado, green creamer, ftd $50, and sugar, ftd $40.

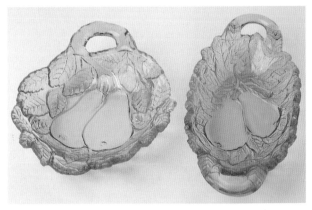

Avocado, green, preserve bowl, handle $32, and bowl, two handles $35.

BEADED BLOCK

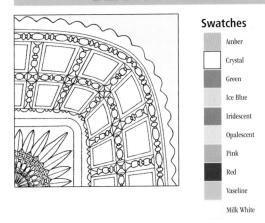

Swatches

- Amber
- Crystal
- Green
- Ice Blue
- Iridescent
- Opalescent
- Pink
- Red
- Vaseline
- Milk White

Manufactured by Imperial Glass Company, Bellaire, Ohio, from 1927 to the 1930s.

Made in amber, crystal, green, ice blue, iridescent, milk white (1950s), opalescent, pink, red, and vaseline. Some pieces are still being made in pink and are embossed with the "IG" trademark. Red is very scarce. The secondary market for milk white is still being established.

Item	Amber	Crystal	Green	Ice Blue
Bowl, 4-1/2" d, lily	$22	$18	$20	$26
Bowl, 4-1/2" d, two handles	18	10	22	28
Bowl, 5-1/2" sq	18	8	20	12

Item	Amber	Crystal	Green	Ice Blue
Bowl, 5-1/2" d, 1 handle	18	8	20	12
Bowl, 6" deep	24	12	24	15
Bowl, 6-1/4" d	24	8.50	20	12
Bowl, 6-1/2" d, two handles	24	8.50	20	12
Bowl, 6-3/4" d	27.50	12	28	14

Beaded Block, ice blue vase $35, and crystal jelly, stemmed $10.

Item	Amber	Crystal	Green	Ice Blue
Bowl, 7-1/4" d, flared	30	12	28	14
Bowl, 7-1/2" d, fluted	30	22	30	24
Bowl, 7-1/2" plain	30	20	30	22
Candy dish, cov, pear shaped	-	-	395	-
Celery, 8-1/4" d	35	18	35	18
Creamer, ftd	25	25	25	24
Jelly, 4-1/2" h, stemmed	20	10	20	12
Jelly, 4-1/2" h, stemmed, flared lid	24	20	24	30
Pitcher, 1 pt, 5-1/4" h	95	115	125	115
Plate, 7-3/4" sq	20	7.50	20	10
Plate, 8-3/4"	30	24	30	30
Sugar, ftd	25	24	30	30
Syrup	-	-	-	-
Vase, 6" h, ftd	25	20	35	35

Additional Colors:

Item	Irid.	Opal	Pink	Vaseline
Bowl, 4-1/2" d, lily	$18	$30	$18	$24
Bowl, 4-1/2" d, two handles	20	30	12	28
Bowl, 5-1/2" sq	10	15	10	12
Bowl, 5 -1/2 d, 1 handle	10	15	20	12
Bowl, 6" deep	12	24	18	15
Bowl, 6-1/4" d	12	18	10	12
Bowl, 6-1/4" d, two handles	12	18	28	12
Bowl, 6-3/4" d	15	20	14	14
Bowl, 7-1/4" d, flared	15	20	14	14
Bowl, 7-1/2" d, fluted	20	24	24	24
Bowl, 7-1/2" plain	24	24	20	22

Beaded Block, 7-1/2" crystal fluted bowl $22.

Item	Irid.	Opal	Pink	Vaseline
Candy dish, cov, pear shaped	-	-	-	650
Celery, 8-1/4" d	18	30	16.50	18
Creamer, ftd	24	50	30	24
Jelly, 4-1/2" h, stemmed	12	15	12	12
Jelly, 4-1/2" h, stemmed, flared lid	15	24	15	12
Pitcher, 1 pt, 5-1/4" h	115	125	195	115
Plate, 7-3/4" sq	10	15	8	10
Plate, 8-3/4"	20	24	20	20
Sugar, ftd	20	60	30	20
Syrup	-	-	-	165
Vase, 6" h, ftd	25	20	36	30

Beaded Block is a very popular pattern with those who collect only Depression glass. It is also popular with those who specialize in collecting patterns made by the Imperial Glass Co., long known for their intricate and interesting patterns and shapes.

Beaded Block, vaseline square plate $10, and iridescent round plate $20.

BLOCK OPTIC

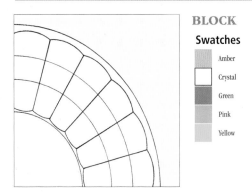

BLOCK

Swatches

Amber

Crystal

Green

Pink

Yellow

Manufactured by Hocking Glass Company, Lancaster, Ohio, from 1929 to 1933.

Made in amber, crystal, green, pink, and yellow. Production in amber was very limited. A 11-3/4" d console bowl is valued at $50, while a pair of matching 1-3/4" h candlesticks is valued at $110.

* There are five styles of creamers and four styles of cups; each has a relative value.

Item	Crystal	Green	Pink	Yellow
Berry bowl, 8-1/2" d	$24	$40	$45	$-
Bowl, 4-1/4" d, 1-3/8" h	6	15	10	-
Bowl, 4-1/2" d, 1-1/2" h	-	28	-	-
Bowl, 8-5/8" d, low, ruffled	-	150	-	-
Butter dish, cov	-	50	-	-
Cake plate, 10" d, ftd	18	-	-	-
Creamer	12	20	18	20

Block Optic, 8-1/2" d green berry bowl, $40, 5-1/4" d look-alike bowl (missing center design) $5, and 4-1/4" d individual berry bowl $15.

Item	Crystal	Green	Pink	Yellow
Candlesticks, pr, 1-3/4" h	-	120	100	-
Candy jar, cov, 2-1/4" h	30	60	55	75
Candy jar, cov, 6-1/4" h	42	80	60	-
Champagne, 4-3/4" h	12.50	30	18.50	24
Cocktail, 4" h	-	35	45	-
Compote, 4" wide	-	36	70	-
Console bowl, 11-3/4" d, rolled	55	75	125	-
Creamer*	12	20	18	20
Cup*	7.50	9	12	12
Goblet, 9 oz, 5-3/4" h	12	40	45	-

Block Optic, 3-1/2" green tumbler $24.

Block Optic, 4-3/4" pink footed sherbet $17.50.

Item	Crystal	Green	Pink	Yellow
Goblet, 9 oz, 7-1/2" h, thin	24	-	30	45
Ice bucket	-	40	48	-
Ice tub, open	-	65	120	-
Pitcher, 54 oz, 7-5/8" h, bulbous	-	95	85	-
Pitcher, 54 oz, 8-1/2" h	25	45	40	-
Pitcher, 80 oz, 8" h	-	90	85	-
Plate, 6" d, sherbet	2.50	7	5	6.50
Plate, 8" d, luncheon	3.50	6	8.50	9.50
Plate, 9" d, dinner	11	35	38	45
Plate, 9" d, dinner, snowflake center	-	16.50	-	-
Plate, 9" d, grill	15	27.50	30	60
Salad bowl, 7-1/4" d	-	155	-	-
Salt and pepper shakers, pr, ftd	-	42	90	95
Salt and pepper shakers, pr, squatty	-	100	-	-
Sandwich plate, 10-1/4" d	-	27.50	30	-
Sandwich server, center handle	-	65	50	-
Saucer, 5-3/4" d	-	12	10	-
Saucer, 6-1/8" d	2	10	10	4
Sherbet, 5-1/2 oz, 3-1/4" h	-	12	9.50	7.50
Sherbet, 6 oz, 4-3/4" h	8	28	17.50	20
Sugar, cone	-	19.50	15	15
Sugar, flat	-	20	10	-
Sugar, round, ftd	10	12	18	16
Tumbler, 3 oz, 2-5/8" h	-	27.50	30	-
Tumbler, 3 oz, 3-1/4" h, ftd	-	27.50	25	-
Tumbler, 5 oz, 3-1/2" h, flat	-	24	20	-
Tumbler, 5-3/8" h, ftd	-	-	24	18
Tumbler, 9" h, ftd	-	-	17.50	22
Tumbler, 9-1/2 oz, 3-13/16" h, flat	-	17.50	15	-
Tumbler, 10 oz, 6" h, ftd	12	-	-	-

Item	Crystal	Green	Pink	Yellow
Tumbler, 10 or 11 oz, 5" h, flat	-	30	35	-
Tumbler, 12 oz, 4-7/8" h, flat	-	35.50	30	-
Tumbler, 15 oz, 5-1/4" h, flat	-	32.50	30	-
Vase, 5-3/4" h, blown	-	350	-	-
Whiskey, 2 oz, 2-1/4" h	15	35	30	-
Wine, 3-1/2" h	-	400	400	-

Block Optic, green sherbet $28, sugar $19.50,
creamer $20, and Hazel Atlas look-alike covered candy dish.

BOWKNOT

Swatches

Green

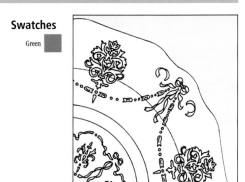

Unknown maker, late 1920s.
Made in green.

Item	Green
Berry bowl, 4-1/2" d	$25
Cereal bowl, 5-1/2" d	30
Cup	20
Plate, 7" d, salad	18
Sherbet, low, ftd	25
Tumbler, 10 oz, 5" h, flat	20
Tumbler, 10 oz, 5" h, ftd	25

Bowknot, green tumbler $25, and footed berry bowl $25.

BUBBLE

BULLSEYE, PROVINCIAL

Swatches

Crystal	
Forest Green	
Pink	
Royal Ruby	
Sapphire Blue	

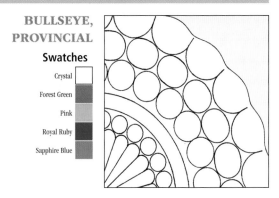

Manufactured originally by Hocking Glass Company, and followed by Anchor Hocking Glass Corporation, Lancaster, Ohio, from 1937 to 1965.

Made in crystal (1937); forest green (1937); pink, Royal Ruby (1963); and sapphire blue (1937). Production in pink was limited. The current value for a pink cup and saucer is $175.

Item	Crystal	Forest Green	Royal Ruby	Sapph. Blue
Berry bowl, 4" d	$4	$-	$6.50	$20
Berry bowl, 8-3/4" d	12	15	15	20
Bowl, 9" d, flanged	8	-	-	335
Candlesticks, pr	18	40	-	-
Cereal bowl, 5-1/4" d	10	20	-	17.50
Cocktail, 3-1/2 oz	4.50	15	18	-
Cocktail, 4-1/2 oz	4.50	16	16	-
Creamer	7.50	15	18	45

Bubble, sapphire blue grill plate $22,
platter $18, soup bowl $16, 4" d berry bowl $20.

Item	Crystal	Forest Green	Royal Ruby	Sapph. Blue
Cup	4.50	9.75	12.50	15
Fruit bowl, 4-1/2" d	5	11	9	12
Goblet, 9 oz, stem, 5-1/2" h	7.50	15	15	-
Goblet, 9-1/2 oz, stem	8	15	18	-
Iced tea goblet, 14 oz	8	17.50	-	-
Iced tea tumbler, 12 oz, 4-1/2" h	12.50	-	19.50	-
Juice goblet, 4 oz	3	14	-	-
Juice goblet, 5-1/2 oz	5	12.50	15	-
Juice tumbler, 6 oz, ftd	4	12	10	-

Item	Crystal	Forest Green	Royal Ruby	Sapph. Blue
Lamp, 3 styles	42	-	-	-
Lemonade Tumbler, 16 oz, 5-7/8" h	16	-	16	-
Old Fashioned Tumbler, 8 oz, 3-1/4" h	6.50	16	16 .50	-
Pitcher, 64 oz, ice lip	60	-	65	-
Plate, 6-3/4" d, bread and butter	4	4.50	-	3.75
Plate, 9-3/8" d, dinner	7.50	28	27.50	10
Plate, 9-3/8" d, grill	-	20	-	22
Platter, 12" l, oval	10	-	-	18
Sandwich Plate, 9-1/2" d	7.50	25	22	8
Saucer	1.50	5	5	1.50
Sherbet, 6 oz	5	9	12	-
Soup Bowl, flat, 7-3/4" d	10	-	-	16
Sugar	6	14.50	-	35
Tidbit, 2 tiers	-	-	35	-
Tumbler, 9 oz, water	6	-	16	-

*Bubble, royal ruby
cup $12.50.*

BY CRACKY

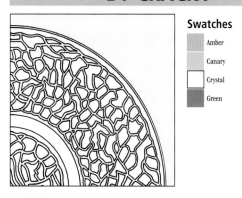

Swatches

Amber

Canary

Crystal

Green

Manufactured by L.E. Smith Glass Company, Mount Pleasant, Pa., in the late 1920s.

Made in amber, canary, crystal, and green.

Item	Amber	Canary	Crystal	Green
Cake plate, ftd	$35	$40	$30	$30
Candleholder, octagonal base	7.50	10	5	5
Candleholder, round base	5	7.50	5	5
Candy box, cov	17.50	20	15	17.50
Candy jar, cov	20	25	17.50	17.50
Center bowl, 12", octagonal	15	17.50	12	15
Cup	5	5	5	5
Goblet	18	18	10	15
Flower block, 3"	15	17.50	7.50	10
Plate, 8"	15	17.50	7.50	10
Saucer	3	5	2	2

Item	Amber	Canary	Crystal	Green
Sherbet	7.50	10	5	5
Sherbet plate	12	15	5	7.50
Vase, fan shape	20	25	15	15
Violet bowl	20	25	15	15

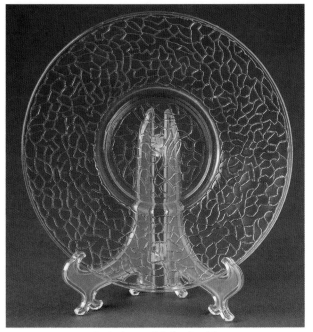

By Cracky, crystal sherbet plate $5.

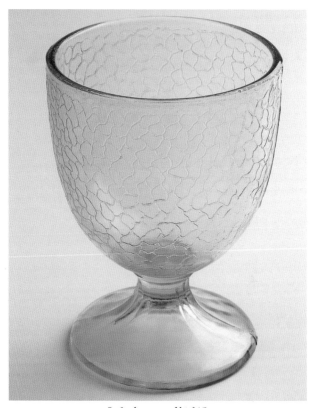

*By Cracky, green goblet **$15**.*

By Cracky, green covered candy **$17.50**.

By Cracky, 4-3/4" green footed cone-shaped goblet **$15**.

CAMEO

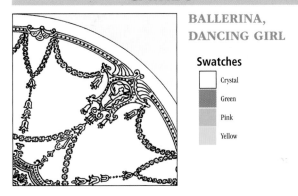

BALLERINA, DANCING GIRL

Swatches

☐	Crystal
■	Green
■	Pink
■	Yellow

Manufactured by Hocking Glass Company, Lancaster, Ohio, from 1930 to 1934.

Made in crystal, green, pink, and yellow. Only the crystal has a platinum rim.

Reproductions: † Salt shakers made in blue, green, and pink. Children's dishes have been made in green and pink, but were never part of the original pattern. Recently, a squatty candy dish in cobalt blue has also been made. This was not an original color.

Item	Crystal	Green	Pink	Yellow
Berry bowl, 8-1/4" d	$-	$48	$175	$-
Butter dish, cov	-	250	-	1,500
Cake plate, 10" d, 3 legs	-	50	-	-
Cake plate, 10-1/2" d, flat	-	120	165	-
Candlesticks, pr, 4" h	-	150	-	-

Cameo, green vegetable bowl $55.

Item	Crystal	Green	Pink	Yellow
Candy jar, cov, 4" h	-	110	495	125
Candy jar, cov, 6-1/2" h	-	195	-	-
Cereal bowl, 5-1/2" d	9.50	45	160	35
Cocktail shaker	600	-	-	-
Comport, 5" w	-	65	200	-
Console bowl, 3 legs, 11" d	-	90	45	125
Cookie jar, cov	-	85	-	-
Cream soup, 4-3/4" d	-	215	-	-
Creamer, 3-1/4" h	-	30	110	25
Creamer, 4-1/4" h	-	30	115	-
Decanter, 10" h	235	225	-	-
Domino tray, 7" l	165	275	265	-
Goblet, 6" h, water	-	95	195	-

*Cameo, 3-1/4"
yellow creamer
$25.*

Cameo, 8" yellow plate $12.50.

Item	Crystal	Green	Pink	Yellow
Ice bowl, 3" h, 5-1/2" d	265	300	750	-
Jam jar, cov, 2" h	185	275	-	-
Juice pitcher, 6" h, 36 oz	-	110	-	-
Juice tumbler, 3 oz, ftd	-	65	90	-
Pitcher, 8-1/2" h, 56 oz	550	70	1,450	-
Plate, 7" d, salad	12	13.50	-	-
Plate, 8" d, luncheon	8	18	36	12.50
Plate, 8-1/2", luncheon, sq	-	70	-	250
Plate, 9-1/2" d, dinner	-	30	85	15
Plate, 10-1/2" d, dinner, rimmed	-	115	175	-
Plate, 10-1/2" d, grill	-	20	55	14.50
Platter, 12" l	-	35	-	42
Relish, 7-1/2" l, ftd, 3 parts	175	40	-	-
Salad bowl, 7-1/4" d	-	70	-	-
Salt and pepper shakers, pr, ftd †	-	95	90	-
Saucer	4	4	90	4.50
Sherbet, 3-1/8" h, blown	-	18	75	-
Sherbet, 3-1/8" h, molded	-	18	75	40
Sherbet, 4-7/8" h	-	40	100	45
Soup bowl, rimmed, 9" d	-	100	135	85
Sugar, 3-1/4" h	-	25	-	22
Sugar, 4-1/4" h	-	32.50	125	-
Syrup pitcher, 20 oz, 5-3/4" h	-	250	-	2,000
Tumbler, 9 oz, 4" h	16	32	80	-
Tumbler, 9 oz, 5" h, ftd	-	30	115	20
Tumbler, 10 oz, 4-3/4" h, flat	-	35	95	-
Tumbler, 11 oz, 5" h, flat	-	30	90	60
Tumbler, 11 oz, 5-3/4" h, ftd	-	75	135	-
Tumbler, 15 oz, 5-1/4" h	-	80	145	-
Tumbler, 15 oz, 6-3/8" h, ftd	-	495	-	-

Item	Crystal	Green	Pink	Yellow
Vase, 5-3/4" h	-	375	-	-
Vase, 8" h	-	75	-	-
Vegetable, oval, 10" l	-	55	-	48
Wine, 3-1/2" h	-	1,200	950	-
Wine, 4" h	-	95	250	-

*Cameo, crystal
tumbler with
platinum trim $16.*

CAPRI

Swatches

Azure Blue

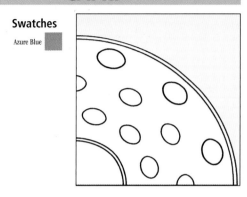

Manufactured by Hazel Ware, division of Continental Can, 1960s. Collectors are starting to divide these wares into several distinct patterns, based on the shape. All are the same pretty azure blue color and have the same market value. Original "Capri" paper labels are found on most of the styles.

Made in azure blue.

Item	Azure Blue
Ashtray, 3-1/2" sq, emb flower center	$15
Ashtray, 3-1/4" w, triangular or round	6
Ashtray, 5" d, round	7.50
Ashtray, 6-7/8" w, triangular	10
Bowl, 4-3/4" d, octagonal or swirled	6.50
Bowl, 4-7/8" d, round, Dots	7.50
Bowl, 5-3/4" w, sq	10

Capri, azure blue covered candy $35.

Capri, 7-3/4" l, azure blue candy dish with metal handle $12.

Capri, 6" azure blue round bowl $6.

Item	Azure Blue
Bowl, 5-5/8", Colony Swirl	6.50
Bowl, 6" d, Dots, Colony Swirl	6
Bowl, 6" d, Tulip	12
Bowl, 7-3/4" l, oval	14
Bowl, 8-3/4" d, swirled	18
Bowl, 9-1/2" d	18
Candy jar, cov, ftd	35
Chip and dip set, metal rack	30
Creamer	12
Cup, octagonal	6.50
Iced tea tumbler, 5" h, 12 oz	10
Old fashioned tumbler, 3-5/8" h, Dots	8.50
Plate, 5-3/4" d, bread and butter	5
Plate, 7" d, salad	6.50
Plate, 8" w, sq	7.50
Plate, 9-3/4", dinner	10
Salad bowl, 5-3/8" d	7.50
Saucer, round, sq, or octagonal	1.50
Sherbet	7.50
Snack plate, fan shape	12
Snack plate, round	9.50
Sugar, cov	20
Tidbit, two bowl tiers, Colony Swirl	45
Tumbler, 2-3/4" h, Colony Swirl	7.50
Tumbler, 3" h, Dots	5.50
Tumbler, 3-1/16", Colony, Colony Swirl	8.50
Tumbler, 4-1/4" h, 9 oz	7.50
Vase, 8" h, Dots	20
Vase, 8-1/2" h, ruffled rim	35

CHERRY BLOSSOM

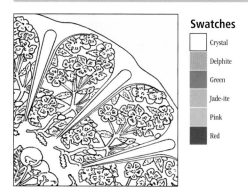

Swatches

☐	Crystal
	Delphite
	Green
	Jade-ite
	Pink
	Red

Manufactured by Jeannette Glass Company, Jeannette, Pa., from 1930 to 1939.

Made in crystal, Delphite, green, jade-ite, pink, and red (production was very limited in crystal, jade-ite and red).

Reproductions: † Reproductions include: small berry bowl, 8-1/2" d bowl, covered butter dish, cake plate, cereal bowl, cup, pitcher, 6" and 9" plates, divided 13" platter, salt shaker, sandwich tray, saucer, and 3-3/4" and 4-1/2" h ftd tumblers. Reproductions have been made in cobalt blue, Delphite, green, pink, and red. A children's butter dish has also been made, which was never included in the original production.

Item	Delphite	Green	Pink
Berry bowl, 4-3/4" d †	$24	$27.50	$25
Berry bowl, 8-1/2" d †	45	55	50
Bowl, 9" d, two handles	27.50	95	48

*Cherry Blossom, pink sugar $30 ($35 **with lid**).*

Item	Delphite	Green	Pink
Butter dish, cov †	-	115	75
Cake plate, 10-1/4" d, 3 legs †	-	38	35
Cereal bowl, 5-3/4" d †	-	35	60
Coaster	-	15	15
Creamer	30	20	25
Cup †	28	28	30
Fruit bowl, 10-1/2" d	32	120	135
Juice tumbler, 1 oz, 3-1/2"	25	35	25
Mug, 7 oz	-	195	265
Pitcher, 36 oz, 6-3/4" h, 36 oz †	95	60	78
Pitcher, 36 oz, 8", PAT, ftd	-	65	75
Pitcher, 42 oz, 8", PAT, flat	-	65	95
Plate, 6" d, sherbet †	12.50	10	12
Plate, 7" d, salad	-	30	28
Plate, 9" d, dinner †	20	24	30
Plate, 9" d, grill	-	35	32.50
Plate, 10" d, grill	-	32.50	-
Platter, 11" l, oval	40	55	50
Platter, 13" d	-	150	150
Platter, 13" divided †	-	72	75
Salt and pepper shakers, pr, scallop base †	-	995	1,250
Sandwich tray, 10-1/2" d †	20	30	45
Saucer †	6	8	6.50
Sherbet	24	30	22
Soup, flat, 7-3/4" d	-	90	80
Sugar, cov	20	27.50	35
Tumbler, 3-3/4" h, AOP, ftd †	-	22	24
Tumbler, 5" h	20	70	72
Tumbler, 8 oz, 4-1/2" h, scalloped ftd base, AOP	-	40	42

Item	Delphite	Green	Pink
Tumbler, 9 oz, 4-1/4" h	-	24	20
Tumbler, 9 oz, 4-1/2" h †	30	30	30
Vegetable bowl, 9" l, oval	45	42	40

Children's

Item	Delphite	Pink
Creamer	$50	$50
Cup †	42	65
Plate, 6" d	15	15
Saucer	7.50	7.50
Sugar	50	50

Cherry Blossom, 11" green oval platter $55.

Cherry Blossom, 4-3/4" d delphite berry bowls, each $24.

CHERRYBERRY

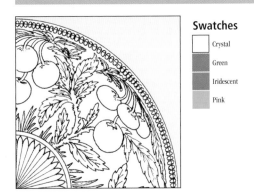

Swatches

☐	Crystal
■	Green
■	Iridescent
■	Pink

Manufactured by U.S. Glass Company, Pittsburgh, Pa., early 1930s. Made in crystal, green, iridescent, and pink.

Item	Crystal	Green	Irid.	Pink
Berry bowl, 4" d	$7	$8.75	$7	$8.75
Berry bowl, 7-1/2" d, deep	19.50	35	22	24
Bowl, 6-1/4" d, 2" deep	50	55	40	55
Butter dish, cov	150	175	150	175
Comport, 5-3/4"	17.50	25	17.50	25
Creamer, large, 4-5/8"	40	45	40	45
Creamer, small	15	20	15	20
Olive dish, 5" l, one handle	10	15	10	15
Pickle dish, 8-1/4" l, oval	10	15	10	15
Pitcher, 7-3/4" h	165	175	165	175
Plate, 6" d, sherbet	6.50	11	6.50	11
Plate, 7-1/2" d, salad	8.50	15	9	15

Item	Crystal	Green	Irid.	Pink
Salad bowl, 6-1/2" d, deep	17.50	22	17.50	22
Sherbet	10	12	12	14
Sugar, large, cov	45	75	45	75
Sugar, small, open	15	20	15	20
Tumbler, 9 oz, 3-5/8" h	20	35	20	35

Cherryberry, 7-1/2" d, deep, crystal berry bowl $19.50.

CHINEX CLASSIC

Swatches

Chinex (Ivory)

Manufactured by Macbeth-Evans Division of Corning Glass Works, from the late 1930s to early 1940s.

Made in Chinex (ivory) and Chinex with Classic Bouquet or Classic Castle decal.

Item	Chinex	Chinex Classic Bouquet decal	Chinex Classic Castle decal
Bowl, 11" d	$20	$36	$48
Butter dish, cov	55	80	135
Cake plate, 11-1/2" d	10	15	25
Cereal bowl, 5- 3/4" d	6	8.50	15
Creamer	5	12	20
Cup	6	9.50	17.50
Plate, 6-1/4" d, sherbet	4	6.50	10
Plate, 9-3/4" d, dinner	5	9	10
Sandwich plate, 11-1/2" d	8.50	12	25

Item	Chinex	Chinex Classic Bouquet decal	Chinex Classic Castle decal
Saucer	2	4	7
Sherbet, low, ftd	9.50	12	30
Soup bowl, 7-3/4" d	14	25	40
Sugar, open	7.50	12.50	20
Vegetable bowl, 7" d	15	25	35
Vegetable bowl, 9" d	15	25	35

Chinex Classic, plate with castle decal $10.

CHRISTMAS CANDY

NO. 624

Swatches

Crystal

Terrace Green

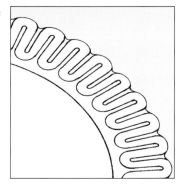

Manufactured by Indiana Glass Company, Dunkirk, Ind., 1950s. Made in crystal and Terrace Green (teal).

Item	Crystal	Terrace Green
Bowl, 5-3/4" d	$6.50	$-
Creamer	17.50	45
Cup	8.50	38
Mayonnaise, ladle, liner	24	-
Plate, 6" d, bread and butter	6	16
Plate, 8-1/4" d, luncheon	8	30
Plate, 9-5/8"d, dinner	12	36
Sandwich plate, 11-1/4" d	24	65
Saucer	5	15

Item	Crystal	Terrace Green
Soup bowl, 7-3/8" d	12	75
Sugar	15	45
Tidbit, two tiers	20	-
Vegetable bowl, 9-1/2" d	-	235

Christmas Candy, crystal sugar $15, and creamer $17.50.

CIRCLE

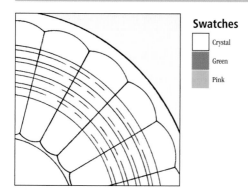

Swatches

☐	Crystal
■	Green
■	Pink

Manufactured by Hocking Glass Company, Lancaster, Ohio, in the 1930s.

Made in crystal, green, and pink. Crystal is listed in the original catalogs, but few pieces have surfaced to date. A crystal 3-1/8" d sherbet is known and valued at $4.

Item	Green	Pink
Bowl, 4-1/2" d	$15	$15
Bowl, 5-1/2" d, flared	17.50	17.50
Bowl, 8" d	16	16
Bowl, 9-3/8" d	18.50	18.50
Creamer, ftd	9	16
Cup	6.50	7.50
Goblet, 8 oz, 5-3/4" h	16.50	15
Iced tea tumbler, 10 oz	17.50	17.50

Item	Green	Pink
Juice tumbler, 4 oz	9.50	9
Pitcher, 60 oz	35	35
Pitcher, 80 oz	30	32
Plate, 6" d, sherbet	6	6
Plate, 8-1/4" d, luncheon	12	12
Plate, 9-1/2" d, dinner	12	12
Sandwich plate, 10" d	15	17.50
Saucer, 6" d	2.50	2.50
Sherbet, 3-1/8"	8	8
Sherbet, 4-3/4"	10	12
Sugar, ftd	12	16
Tumbler, 8 oz	10	10
Tumbler, 15 oz, flat	17.50	17.50
Wine, 4-1/2" h	15	15

Circle, green cup $6.50.

CLOVERLEAF

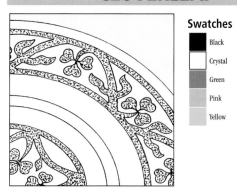

Swatches

- ■ Black
- □ Crystal
- ▨ Green
- ▨ Pink
- ▨ Yellow

Manufactured by Hazel Atlas Glass Company, Clarksburg, W.V., and Zanesville, Ohio, from 1930 to 1936.

Made in black, crystal, green, pink, and yellow. Collector interest in crystal is minimal; prices are about 50 percent of those listed for green.

Item	Black	Green	Pink	Yellow
Ashtray, match holder, 4" d	$65	$-	$-	$-
Ashtray, match holder, 5-3/4" d	90	-	-	-
Bowl, 8" d	-	95	-	-
Candy dish, cov	-	65	-	130
Cereal bowl, 5" d	-	50	-	55
Creamer, 3-5/8" h, ftd	25	12	-	24
Cup	20	12	8	12
Dessert bowl, 4" d	-	30	30	35
Plate, 6" d, sherbet	40	6.50	-	10

*Cloverleaf, 4" green flat tumbler $65, and
green 5-3/4" cone-shaped footed tumbler $50.*

Item	Black	Green	Pink	Yellow
Plate, 8" d, luncheon	18	15	12	18
Salad bowl, 7" d	-	60	-	65
Salt and pepper shakers, pr	100	40	-	140
Saucer	10	10	7	5
Sherbet, 3" h, ftd	22	25	10	16
Sugar, 3-5/8" h, ftd	25	12	-	24
Tumbler, 9 oz, 4" h, flat	-	65	26.50	35
Tumbler, 10 oz, 3-3/4" h, flat	-	50	30	-
Tumbler, 10 oz, 5-3/4" h, ftd	-	50	-	40

Cloverleaf, green saucer $10, pink plate $12, and pink cup $8.

COLONIAL

KNIFE AND FORK

Swatches

Crystal

Green

Pink

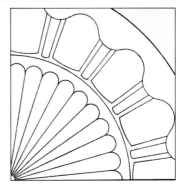

Manufactured by Hocking Glass Company, Lancaster, Ohio, from 1934 to 1938.

Made in crystal, green, and pink.

Item	Crystal	Green	Pink
Berry bowl, 3-3/4" d	$-	$-	$60
Berry bowl, 4-1/2"	10	20	18
Berry bowl, 9" d	24	36	35
Butter dish, cov	45	60	700
Cereal bowl, 5-1/2" d	32	85	60
Claret, 4 oz, 5-1/4" h	21	31.50	-
Cocktail, 3 oz, 4" h	15	27.50	-
Cordial, 1 oz, 3-3/4" h	25	30	-
Cream soup bowl, 4-1/2" d	70	85	72
Creamer, 8 oz, 5" h	20	25	65
Cup	8	15	12

Colonial, green covered butter $60.

Item	Crystal	Green	Pink
Goblet, 8-1/2 oz, 5-3/4" h	20	36	40
Ice tea tumbler, 12 oz	28	55	45
Juice tumbler, 5 oz, 3" h	17.50	27.50	24.50
Lemonade tumbler, 15 oz	47.50	75	65
Milk pitcher, 8 oz, 5" h	25	25	65
Mug, 12 oz, 5-1/2" h	-	825	500
Pitcher, 54 oz, 7" h, ice lip	40	45	48
Pitcher, 54 oz, 7" h, no lip	40	45	48
Pitcher, 68 oz, 7-3/4" h, ice lip	35	72	65
Pitcher, 68 oz, 7-3/4" h, no lip	45	72	65
Plate, 6" d, sherbet	4.50	10	7
Plate, 8-1/2" d, luncheon	6	8	10
Plate, 10" d, dinner	35	67.50	65

Colonial, green creamer $25, and sugar $12.

Item	Crystal	Green	Pink
Plate, 10" d, grill	**17.50**	30	27.50
Plate, 12" d, oval	**17.50**	25	30
Platter, 12" l, oval	**17.50**	25	35
Salt and pepper shakers, pr	**60**	160	150
Saucer	**4.50**	7.50	6.50
Sherbet, 3" h	-	-	24
Sherbet, 3-3/8" h	**10**	18	12
Soup bowl, 7" d	**30**	85	85
Spoon holder or celery vase	**105**	130	135
Sugar, cov	**90**	55	50
Sugar, 5", open	**10**	12	15
Tumbler, 3 oz, 3-1/4" h, ftd	**18**	20	16.50
Tumbler, 5 oz, 4" h, ftd	**15**	35	24.50

Colonial, crystal wine $18, and cocktail $15.

Item	Crystal	Green	Pink
Tumbler, 9 oz, 4" h	15	20	25
Tumbler, 10 oz, 5-1/4" h, ftd	30	48.50	50
Tumbler, 11 oz, 5-1/8" h	25	37.50	45
Vegetable bowl, 10" l, oval	18	25	30
Whiskey, 2-1/2" h, 1-1/2 oz	9	20	18
Wine, 4-1/2" h, 2-1/2 oz	18	30	15

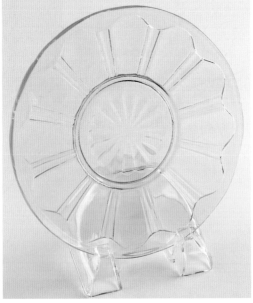

*Colonial,
green
saucer
$7.50.*

Colonial, pink divided grill plate $27.50.

COLONIAL BLOCK

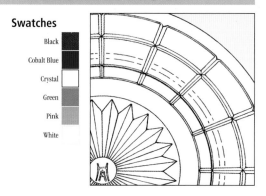

Swatches

Black
Cobalt Blue
Crystal
Green
Pink
White

Manufactured by Hazel Atlas Glass Company, Clarksburg, W.V., and Zanesville, Ohio, early 1930s.

Made in black, cobalt blue (rare), crystal, green, pink, and white (1950s).

Item	Black	Crystal	Green	Pink	White
Bowl, 4" d	$-	$6	$10	$10	$-
Bowl, 7" d	-	16	35	20	-
Butter dish, cov	-	35	50	45	-
Butter tub, cov	-	35	40	40	-
Candy jar, cov	-	30	45	40	-
Compote, 4" h, 4-3/4" w	-	12	-	-	-
Creamer	-	15	16	15	7.50
Goblet, 5-3/4" h	-	9	12	15	-
Pitcher, 20 oz, 5-3/4" h	-	40	50	50	-
Powder jar, cov	30	20	24	24	-

Item	Black	Crystal	Green	Pink	White
Sherbet	-	6	10	9.50	-
Sugar, cov	-	20	25	25	20
Sugar, open	-	10	8	8	10

Colonial Block, green covered butter dish $50.

COLONIAL FLUTED

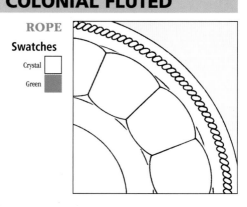

ROPE

Swatches

Crystal

Green

Manufactured by Federal Glass Company, Columbus, Ohio, from 1928 to 1933.

Made in crystal and green.

Item	Crystal	Green
Berry bowl, 4" d	$11	$12
Berry bowl, 7-1/2" d	16	30
Cereal bowl, 6" d	15	18
Creamer, ftd	12	14
Cup	5	7.50
Plate, 6" d, sherbet	2.50	4.50
Plate, 8" d, luncheon	5	10
Salad bowl, 6-1/2" d, 2-1/2" deep	22	35
Saucer	2.50	4
Sugar, cov	21	25
Sugar, open	8	10

Colonial Fluted, green open sugar $10, and creamer $14.

Colonial Fluted, 4" green berry bowl $12, and 6" green cereal bowl $18.

COLUMBIA

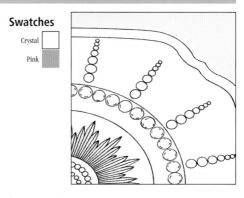

Swatches

Crystal

Pink

Manufactured by Federal Glass Company, Columbus, Ohio, from 1938 to 1942.

Made in crystal and pink. Several flashed (stained) colors are found, and some decaled pieces are known.

Reproductions: † The 2-7/8" h juice tumbler has been reproduced. Look for the "France" on the base to clearly identify the reproductions.

Item	Crystal	Flashed	Pink
Bowl, 10-1/2" d, ruffled edge	$20	$20	$-
Butter dish, cov	22	25	-
Cereal bowl, 5" d	18.50	-	-
Chop plate, 11" d	17	12	-
Crescent-shaped salad	27	-	-
Cup	8.50	10	25

Columbia, crystal covered butter $22.

Item	Crystal	Flashed	Pink
Juice tumbler, 4 oz, 2-3/4" h †	30	-	-
Plate, 6" d, bread & butter	5	4	14
Plate, 9-1/2" d, luncheon	15	12	32
Salad bowl, 8-1/2" d	20	-	-
Saucer	4.50	4	10
Snack tray, cup	30	-	-
Soup bowl, 8" d, low	25	-	-
Tumbler, 9 oz	32.50	-	-

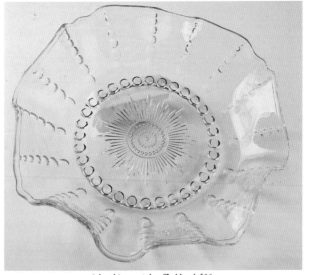

Columbia, crystal ruffled bowl $20.

CORONATION

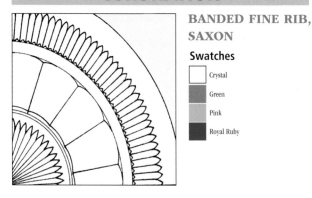

BANDED FINE RIB, SAXON

Swatches

☐	Crystal
■	Green
■	Pink
■	Royal Ruby

Manufactured by Hocking Glass Company, Lancaster, Ohio, from 1936 to 1940.

Made in crystal, green, pink, and Royal Ruby.

Item	Crystal	Green	Pink	Royal Ruby
Berry bowl, 4-1/4" d	$-	$50	$9	$9.50
Berry bowl, 8" d, handle	-	-	18	20
Berry bowl, 8" d	-	195	-	-
Cup	5	-	6	7.50
Nappy bowl, 6-1/2" d	15	-	7.50	15
Pitcher, 68 oz, 7-3/4" h	-	-	500	-
Plate, 6" d, sherbet	2	-	5	-
Plate, 8-1/2" d, luncheon	5	60	15	8.50

Item	Crystal	Green	Pink	Royal Ruby
Saucer	2	-	5	-
Sherbet	-	85	7	-
Tumbler, 10 oz, 5" h, ftd	-	195	35	-

Coronation, ruby handled berry bowl $20.

CRACKED ICE

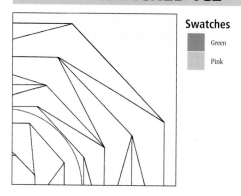

Swatches

▉ Green

▉ Pink

Manufactured by Indiana Glass, Dunkirk, Ind., in the 1930s.

Made in pink and green. Often mistaken for Tea Room, look for the additional diagonal line, giving it a more Art Deco style.

Item	Green	Pink
Creamer	$30	$35
Plate, 6-1/2" d	15	18
Sherbet	12	15
Sugar, cov	30	35
Tumbler	30	32.50

Cracked Ice, pink creamer $35, and covered sugar $35.

CREMAX

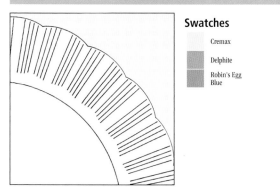

Swatches

Cremax

Delphite

Robin's Egg Blue

Manufactured by Macbeth-Evans Division of Corning Glass Works, late 1930s to early 1940s.

Made in Cremax, Cremax with fired-on colors, Delphite, Robin's Egg Blue, and Bordette. Bordette has a Cremax center with a colored edge.

Item	Bordette	Cremax	Cremax Fired-On	Delphite	Robin's Egg Blue
Cereal bowl, 5-3/4" d	$5	$6	$9	$10	$10
Creamer	6	6.50	6	11	11
Cup	5	5	8	7	7
Demitasse cup	10	20	24	26	26
Demitasse saucer	6	8	10	12	20
Egg cup, 2-1/4" h	12	-	-	-	-
Plate, 6-1/4" d, bread and butter	4	4	5.50	7	7

Item	Bordette	Cremax	Cremax Fired-On	Delphite	Robin's Egg Blue
Plate, 9-3/4" d, dinner	14	7	11	12	12
Sandwich plate, 11-1/2" d	9.50	10	15	17	17
Saucer	3.50	4	4	6	6
Sugar, open	6	6.50	6	11	11
Vegetable bowl, 9" d	10	11	10	20	20

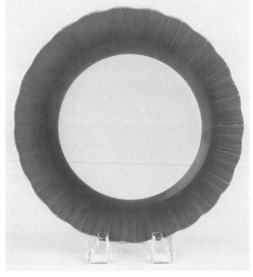

Cremax, dinner plate, Bordette, blue edge $14.

CUBE

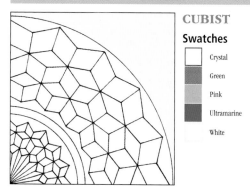

Manufactured by Jeannette Glass Company, Jeannette, Pa., from 1929 to 1933.

Made in amber, crystal, green, pink, ultramarine, and white. Production in amber and white is limited to the 2-3/8" h sugar bowl, and is valued at $3.

Item	Crystal	Green	Pink	Ultramarine
Bowl, 4-1/2" d, deep	$-	$7	$10	$35
Butter dish, cov	-	95	100	-
Candy jar, cov, 6-1/2" h	-	55	40	-
Coaster, 3-1/4" d	-	10	10	-
Creamer, 2-5/8" h	5	10	12	70
Creamer, 3-9/16" h	-	9	9	-
Cup	-	7	8	-
Dessert bowl, 4-1/2" d, pointed rim	4	8.50	9.50	-

Cube, green covered powder jar $30.

Cube, green berry bowl $7, green coaster $10, and green sherbet $8.50.

Item	Crystal	Green	Pink	Ultramarine
Pitcher, 8-3/4" h, 45 oz	-	265	215	-
Plate, 8" d, luncheon	-	8.50	7.50	-
Powder Jar, cov, 3 legs	-	30	30	-
Salt and Pepper Shakers, pr	-	40	36	-
Saucer	1.50	3	4.50	
Sherbet, ftd	-	8.50	12	-
Sugar, cov, 2-3/8" h	4	24	6	
Sugar, cov, 3" h	-	35	25	
Sugar, open, 3"	5	8	7	-
Tumbler, 9 oz, 4" h	-	70	65	

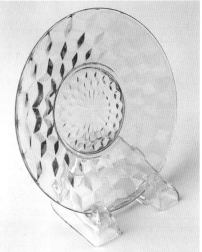

Cube, pink luncheon plate $7.50.

CUPID

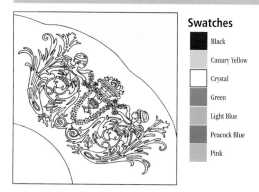

Swatches

■	Black
	Canary Yellow
□	Crystal
■	Green
	Light Blue
■	Peacock Blue
	Pink

Manufactured by Paden City Glass Company, Paden City, W.V., 1930s.

Made in amber, black, canary yellow, crystal, green, light blue, peacock blue, and pink. Prices for colors like amber, black, canary yellow, and light blue are still being established as more pieces of this pattern arrive on the secondary market. This expensive pattern is one to keep your eyes open for while searching at flea markets and garage sales.

Item	Crystal	Green	Peacock Blue	Pink
Bowl, 8-1/2" l, oval, ftd	$-	$300	$-	$450
Bowl, 9-1/4" d, center handle	-	275	-	275
Bowl, 10-1/2" d, rolled edge	-	275	-	250
Cake plate, 11-3/4" h	-	200	-	200

Item	Crystal	Green	Peacock Blue	Pink
Cake stand, 2" h, ftd	-	235	-	235
Candlesticks, pr, 5" h	-	245	-	245
Candy, cov, 3 part	-	385	-	385
Candy, cov, 5-1/4" h	-	295	-	295
Champagne, 5-7/8" h	35	-	-	-
Cocktail, 5-1/8" h	25	-	-	-
Comport, 4-1/2" h, ftd	-	175	-	175
Comport, 6-1/4" h, ftd	-	185	225	325
Console bowl, 11" d	-	250	-	250
Creamer, 4-1/2" h, ftd	45	150	-	150
Creamer, 5" h, ftd	-	150	-	150
Fruit bowl, 9-1/4" d, ftd	-	360	-	360
Fruit bowl, 10-1/4" d	-	245	-	275
Ice bucket, 6" h	-	325	-	325
Ice tub, 4-3/4" h	-	325	-	325
Mayonnaise, 6" d, spoon, 8" d plate	-	275	295	275
Plate, 10-1/2" d	-	150	175	150
Samovar	-	990	-	990
Sugar, 4-1/4" h, ftd	-	150	-	200
Sugar, 5" h, ftd	-	150	-	150
Tray, 10-3/4" d, center handle	-	225	-	200
Tray, 10-7/8" l, oval, ftd	-	250	-	250
Vase, 8-1/4" h, elliptical	-	650	-	650
Vase, 10" h	-	315	-	315
Wine, 5-1/8" h	12.50	-	-	-

Cupid, 6-1/4" h pink low pedestal-foot comport, $325.

DAISY

NO. 620

Swatches

Amber

Crystal

Dark Green

Milk White

Manufactured by Indiana Glass Company, Dunkirk, Ind., from late 1930s to 1980s.

Made in amber (1940s), crystal (1933-40), dark green (1960s-80s), fired-on red (late 1930s), and milk glass (1960s-80s).

Item	Amber or Fired-On Red	Crystal or Milk White	Dark Green
Berry bowl, 4-1/2" d	$12	$6	$6
Berry bowl, 7-3/8" d, deep	15.50	8.50	12.50
Berry bowl, 9-3/8" d, deep	35	26	14
Cake plate, 11-1/2" d	16.50	12	14
Cereal bowl, 6" d	25	10	10
Cream soup bowl, 4-1/2" d	12.50	7.50	12.50
Creamer, ftd	10	8	5
Cup	6	4	6
Plate, 6" d, sherbet	3	4.50	5

Item	Amber or Fired-On Red	Crystal or Milk White	Dark Green
Plate, 7-3/8" d, salad	8.50	8.50	9
Plate, 8-3/8" d, luncheon	6	10	12
Plate, 9-3/8" d, dinner	9	12	10
Plate, 10-3/8" d, grill	15	5.50	18
Platter, 10-3/4" d	16	11	15
Relish dish, 8-3/8" d, 3 part	24	12	12
Sandwich plate, 11-1/2" d	16.50	6	14

Daisy, amber creamer $10.

Item	Amber or Fired-On Red	Crystal or Milk White	Dark Green
Saucer	5	6	5
Sherbet, ftd	10	5	10
Sugar, ftd	10	8	10
Tumbler, 9 oz, ftd	16	10	10
Tumbler, 12 oz, ftd	40	15	22
Vegetable bowl, 10" l, oval	20	18	18

Daisy, green luncheon plate $12.

*Daisy, crystal
luncheon plate $10.*

*Daisy, amber
luncheon plate $6.*

DELLA ROBBIA

#1058

Swatches

Crystal ☐

Manufactured by Westmoreland Glass Company, Grapeville, Pa., from late 1920s to 1940s.

Made in crystal, with applied luster colors and milk glass. Examples of milk white prices are: hand-painted decorated candy jar, $45; creamer, $18; goblet, $20; tumbler, $22.50; wine, $18.

Item	Crystal
Basket, 9"	**$210**
Basket, 12"	**300**
Bowl, 8" d, bell, handle	48
Bowl, 8" d, heart shape, handle	95
Bowl, 12" d, ftd	12
Bowl, 13" d, rolled edge	115
Bowl, 14" d, oval, flange	155
Bowl, 15" d, bell	175
Cake salver, 14" d, ftd	120

Item	Crystal
Candlesticks, pr, 4" h	65
Candlesticks, pr, 4" h, two-lite	350
Candy jar, cov, scalloped edge	150
Champagne, 6 oz	25
Chocolate candy, round, flat	75
Cocktail, 3-1/4 oz	15
Comport, 12" d, ftd, bell	115
Comport, 13" d, flanged	125
Creamer, ftd	18
Cup, coffee	18.50
Finger bowl, 5" d	30
Ginger ale tumbler, 5 oz	25
Goblet, 8 oz, 6" h	30
Iced tea tumbler 11 oz, ftd	35
Iced tea tumbler 12 oz, 5-3/16" h, straight	40
Iced tea tumbler, 12 oz, bell	32
Iced tea tumbler, 12 oz, bell, ftd	32
Mint comport, 6-1/2" d, 3-5/8" h, ftd	45
Nappy, 7-1/2" d	42
Nappy, 8" d, bell	45
Nappy, 4-1/2" d	30
Nappy, 6" d, bell	35
Nappy, 6-1/2" d, one handle	32
Nappy, 9" d	60
Pitcher, 32 oz	200
Plate, 6" d, finger bowl liner	12
Plate, 6-1/8" d, bread and butter	14
Plate, 7-1/4" d, salad	22
Plate, 9" d, luncheon	35
Plate, 10-1/2" d, dinner	95

Item	Crystal
Plate, 18" d	195
Platter, 14" l, oval	195
Punch bowl, 14" d	225
Punch bowl liner, 18" d plate, upturned edge	200
Punch cup	15
Salt and pepper shakers, pr	55
Saucer	10
Sherbet, 5 oz, low foot	22
Sherbet, 5 oz, 4-3/4" h, ftd	24
Sugar, ftd	27.50
Sweetmeat comport, 8" d	115
Torte plate, 14" d	125

*Della Robbia,
crystal salad plate $22.*

Item	Crystal
Tumbler 8 oz, ftd	30
Tumbler, 8 oz, water	32
Wine, 3 oz	25

Della Robbia, luster-decorated compote $125.

DEWDROP

Swatches

Crystal

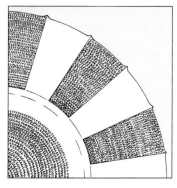

Manufactured by Jeannette Glass Company, Jeannette, Pa., from 1953 to 1956.

Made in crystal. Limited production in irisdescent.

Item	Crystal
Bowl, 4-3/4" d	$9
Bowl, 8-1/2" d	22
Bowl, 10-3/8" d	24
Butter, cov	32
Candy dish, cov, 7" d	30
Casserole, cov	27.50
Creamer	8.50
Iced tea tumbler, 15 oz	17.50
Lazy Susan, 13" d tray	30
Pitcher, 1/2 gallon, ftd	48
Plate, 11-1/2" d	20

Item	Crystal
Punch cup	4
Punch bowl set, bowl, 12 cups	90
Snack cup	4
Snack plate, indent for cup	8
Relish, leaf-shape, handle	9
Sugar, cov	14
Tray, 10" d	22
Tumbler, 9 oz	15

Dewdrop, crystal open sugar $8.50, and creamer $8.50.

Dewdrop, crystal tumbler $15, and iridescent pitcher $50.

DIAMOND QUILTED

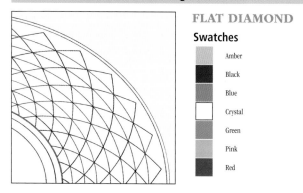

FLAT DIAMOND

Swatches

- Amber
- Black
- Blue
- Crystal
- Green
- Pink
- Red

Manufactured by Imperial Glass Company, Bellaire, Ohio, from late 1920 to early 1930s.

Made in amber, black, blue, crystal, green, pink, and red. Amber and red prices are valued slightly higher than black.

Item	Black	Blue	Crystal
Bowl, 5-1/2" d, one handle	$20	$-	$-
Bowl, 7" d, crimped edge	22	-	-
Cake salver, 10" d, tall	-	-	-
Candlesticks, pr	60	-	50
Candy jar, cov, ftd	-	-	25
Cereal bowl, 5" d	15	-	8
Champagne, 9 oz, 6" h	-	-	-
Compote, 6" h, 7-1/4" w	-	-	-
Compote, cov, 11-1/2" d	-	-	-
Console bowl, 10-1/2" d, rolled edge	65	60	15

Item	Black	Blue	Crystal
Cordial, 1 oz	-	-	-
Cream soup bowl, 4-3/4" d	22	20	20
Creamer	18.50	20	15
Cup	18	18.50	7
Ice bucket	90	90	-
Iced tea tumbler, 12 oz	-	-	-
Mayonnaise set, comport, plate, ladle	60	65	25
Pitcher, 64 oz	-	-	-
Plate, 6" d, sherbet	10	9	7.50
Plate, 7" d, salad	10	10	8
Plate, 8" d, luncheon	12	16	9
Punch bowl and stand	-	-	-
Sandwich plate, 14" d	-	-	-
Sandwich server, center handle	50	50	20
Saucer	5	5	2
Sherbet	16	16	14
Sugar	20	25	12
Tumbler, 6 oz, ftd	-	-	-
Tumbler, 9 oz	-	-	-
Tumbler, 9 oz, ftd	-	-	-
Tumbler, 12 oz, ftd	-	-	-
Vase, fan	80	75	-
Whiskey, 1-1/2 oz	-	-	-
Wine, 2 oz	-	-	-
Wine, 3 oz	-	-	-

Diamond Quilted, 5" green cereal bowl $9.

Diamond Quilted, 8" green plate $6.50.

Additional Colors

Item	Green	Pink
Bowl, 5-1/2" d, one handle	$15	$18
Bowl, 7" d, crimped edge	20	25
Cake salver, 10" d, tall	60	65
Candlesticks, pr	30	28
Candy jar, cov, ftd	65	65
Cereal bowl, 5" d	9	8.50
Champagne, 9 oz, 6" h	12	-
Compote, 6" h, 7-1/4" w	45	48
Compote, cov, 11-1/2" d	80	75

Diamond Quilted, pink sugar $12, and creamer $14.

Item	Green	Pink
Console bowl, 10-1/2" d, rolled edge	20	40
Cordial, 1 oz	12	15
Cream soup bowl, 4-3/4" d	20	14
Creamer	12	14
Cup	10	12
Ice bucket	50	50
Iced tea tumbler, 12 oz	10	10
Mayonnaise set, comport, plate, ladle	37.50	40
Pitcher, 64 oz	50	55
Plate, 6" d, sherbet	7	7.50
Plate, 7" d, salad	8.50	8.50
Plate, 8" d, luncheon	6.50	8.50
Punch bowl and stand	450	450
Sandwich plate, 14" d	15	15
Sandwich server, center handle	25	25
Saucer	4	4
Sherbet	10	10
Sugar	12.50	12
Tumbler, 6 oz, ftd	9	10
Tumbler, 9 oz	14	16
Tumbler, 9 oz, ftd	14	16
Tumbler, 12 oz, ftd	15	15
Vase, fan	50	50
Whiskey, 1-1/2 oz	10	12
Wine, 2 oz	12.50	12.50
Wine, 3 oz	15	15

DIANA

Swatches

Amber

Crystal

Pink

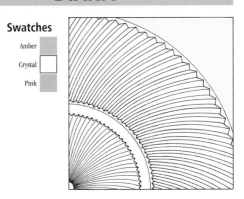

Manufactured by Federal Glass Company, Columbus, Ohio, from 1937 to 1941.

Made in amber, crystal, and pink.

Reproductions: † A 13-1/8" d scalloped pink bowl has been made, which was not original to the pattern.

Item	Amber	Crystal	Pink
Ashtray, 3-1/2" d	$-	$4	$5
Bowl, 12" d, scalloped edge	20	15	32.50
Candy jar, cov, round	40	18.50	48
Cereal bowl, 5" d	15	6.50	15
Coaster, 3-1/2" d	12	4	8
Console/fruit bowl, 11" d	12	20	44
Cream soup bowl, 5-1/2" d	18	14	24
Creamer, oval	12	5	12.50
Cup	7	4	19

Item	Amber	Crystal	Pink
Junior set, six cups and saucers, rack	-	125	300
Plate, 6" d, bread and butter	3.50	2	9.50
Plate, 9-1/2" d, dinner	9	6	18.50
Platter, 12" l, oval	16.50	12	28
Salad bowl, 9" d	18	15	30
Salt and pepper shakers, pr	100	30	75
Sandwich plate, 11-3/4" d	15	9.50	28
Saucer	2.25	2	5
Sherbet	12	7	12
Sugar, open, oval	12	10	16
Tumbler, 9 oz, 4-1/8" h	30	18	45

*Diana, pink
sherbet $12.*

Diana, 5" pink cereal bowl, $15, and 9" pink salad bowl $30.

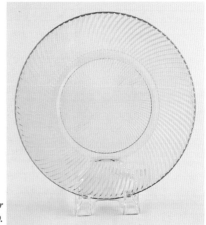

Diana, 9-1/2" pink dinner plate $18.50.

Diana, crystal tumbler $18.

DOGWOOD

Swatches

Cremax

Crystal

Green

Monax

Pink

Yellow

Manufactured by Macbeth-Evans Company, Charleroi, Pa., from 1929 to 1932.

Made in Cremax, crystal, green, Monax, pink and yellow. Yellow is rare; a cereal bowl is known and valued at $95. Crystal items are valued at 50 percent less than green.

Item	Cremax or Monax	Green	Pink
Berry bowl, 8-1/2" d	$40	$100	$65
Cake plate, 11" d, heavy solid foot	-	-	650
Cake plate, 13" d, heavy solid foot	185	135	165
Cereal bowl, 5-1/2" d	12	35	35
Coaster, 3-1/4" d	-	-	450
Creamer, 2-1/2" h, thin	-	48	35
Creamer, 3-1/4" h, thick	-	-	25
Cup, thin	-	32	20

Item	Cremax or Monax	Green	Pink
Cup, thick	36	40	20
Fruit bowl, 10-1/4" d	100	250	550
Pitcher, 8" h, 80 oz (American Sweetheart style)	-	-	1,250
Pitcher, 8" h, 80 oz, decorated	-	550	295
Plate, 6" d, bread and butter	25	10	10
Plate, 8" d, luncheon	-	12	12
Plate, 9-1/4" d, dinner	-	-	45
Plates, 10-1/2" d, grill, AOP or border design only	-	24	35
Platter, 12" d, oval	-	-	725
Salver, 12" d	175	-	45
Saucer	20	10	8.50
Sherbet, low, ftd	-	95	42
Sugar, 2-1/2" h, thin	-	50	30
Sugar, 3-1/4" h, thick, ftd	-	-	20
Tidbit, 2 tier	-	-	90
Tumbler, 10 oz, 4" h, decorated	-	100	55
Tumbler, 11 oz, 4-3/4" h, decorated	-	95	125
Tumbler, 12 oz, 5" h, decorated	-	125	75
Tumbler, molded band	-	-	25

Dogwood, pink sugar $20, creamer $25, and luncheon plate $12.

DORIC

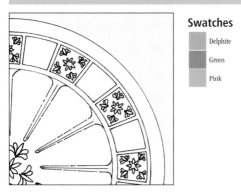

Swatches

- Delphite
- Green
- Pink

Manufactured by Jeannette Glass Company, Jeannette, Pa., from 1935 to 1938.

Made in Delphite, green, pink, and yellow. Yellow is rare.

Item	Delphite	Green	Pink
Berry bowl, 4-1/2" d	$50	$10	$12
Berry bowl, 8-1/4" d	150	38	35
Bowl, 9" d, two handles	-	45	45
Butter dish, cov	-	90	75
Cake plate, 10" d, three legs	-	30	30
Cereal bowl, 5-1/2" d	-	65	90
Coaster, 3" d	-	28	20
Cream soup, 5" d, two handles	-	385	-
Creamer, 4" h	-	17	14
Cup	-	10	10
Pitcher, 36 oz, 6" h, flat	1,200	75	45

Item	Delphite	Green	Pink
Plate, 6" d, sherbet	-	7.50	7.50
Plate, 9" d, dinner	-	24	20
Plate, 9" d, grill	-	20	30
Platter, 12" l, oval	-	32	35
Relish tray, 4" x 8"	-	20	17.50
Salt and pepper shakers, pr	-	40	45
Saucer	-	7	5
Sherbet, footed	12	17.50	15
Sugar, cov	-	35	32
Tumbler, 9 oz, 4-1/2" h, flat	-	100	75
Tumbler, 12 oz, 5" h, ftd.	-	125	85
Vegetable bowl, 9" l, oval	-	45	50

Doric,
green cake plate $30.

DORIC & PANSY

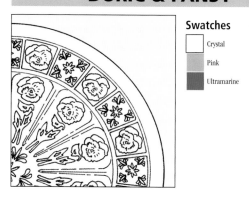

Swatches

Crystal

Pink

Ultramarine

Manufactured by Jeannette Glass Company, Jeannette, Pa., from 1937 to 1938.

Made in ultramarine, with limited production in pink and crystal.

Item	Crystal	Pink	Ultramarine
Berry bowl, 4-1/2" d	$12	$12	$25
Berry bowl, 8" d	-	24	75
Bowl, 9" d, handle	15	20	35
Butter dish, cov	-	-	600
Candy, cov, three parts	-	-	22.50
Cup	12	14	20
Creamer	72	90	145
Plate, 6" d, sherbet	8	12	22
Plate, 7" d, salad	-	-	40
Plate, 9" d, dinner	7.50	8	30
Salt shaker, orig top	-	-	325

Item	Crystal	Pink	Ultramarine
Saucer	4.50	4.50	5.50
Sugar, open	80	85	145
Tray, 10" l, handles	45	-	35
Tumbler, 9 oz, 4-1/2" h	-	-	500

Doric and Pansy, pink dinner plate $8.

Children's

Item	Pink	Ultramarine
Creamer	$42	$50
Cup	35	48
Plate	12	12.50
Saucer	7	8.50
Sugar	35	50
14-pc set, orig box	400	425

Doric and Pansy, ultramarine, child's sugar $50, and creamer $50.

EARLY AMERICAN PRESCUT

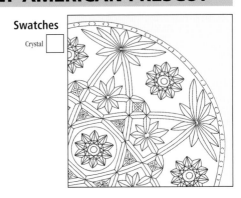

Swatches

Crystal

Manufactured by Anchor Hocking, Lancaster, Ohio, from 1960 to 1999. Made in crystal, with some limited production in colors.

Item	Crystal
Ashtray, 4" d	**$4**
Ashtray, 5" d	8
Ashtray, 7-3/4" d	12
Basket, 6" x 4-1/2"	20
Bowl, 4-1/4" d, plain rim	20
Bowl, 4-1/4" d, scalloped	7.50
Bowl, 5-1/4" d, scalloped	7.50
Bowl, 6-3/4" d, three legs	5
Bowl, 7-1/4" d, scalloped	20
Bowl, 8-3/4" d	9
Bowl, 9" d, oval	8
Bowl, 11-3/4" d, paneled	225

Early American Prescut, crystal covered sugar $4.50, and creamer $3.50.

Item	Crystal
Bud vase, 5" h, ftd	475
Butter, cov, 1/4 lb	7.50
Butter, cov, metal handle, knife	15
Cake plate	25
Candlesticks, pr, two-lite	28.50
Candy, cov, 5-1/4"	12
Candy, cov, 7-1/4"	14.50
Chip and dip, 10-1/4" bowl, metal holder	25
Coaster	6
Cocktail shaker, 30 oz	300
Console bowl, 9" d	15
Creamer	3.50
Deviled egg plate, 11-3/4" d	35
Hostess tray, 6-1/2" x 12"	14
Iced tea tumbler, 15 oz, 6" h	20
Juice tumbler, 5 oz, 4" h	5
Lamp, oil	335
Lazy Susan, 9 pcs	60
Pitcher, 18 oz	15
Pitcher, 40 oz, sq	60
Plate, 6-3/4" d, salad	55
Plate, 6-3/4" d, snack, ring for cup	40
Plate, 10" d, snack	10
Plate, 11" d	15
Punch cup	3
Punch set, 15 pcs	35
Relish, two parts, 10" l, tab handle	7.50
Relish, three parts, 8-1/2" l, oval	6.50
Relish, five parts, 13-1/2" d	30
Salad bowl, 10-3/4" d	15

Item	Crystal
Salt and pepper shakers, pr, individual size	75
Salt and pepper shakers, pr, metal tops	10
Salt and pepper shakers, pr, plastic tops	12
Serving plate, 11" d, four parts	90
Serving plate, 13-1/2" d	15
Sherbet, 6 oz	90
Snack cup	3
Sugar, cov	4.50
Syrup pitcher, 12 oz	24
Tumbler, 10 oz, 4-1/2" h	6.50
Vase, 10" h	15

Early American Prescut, 11" d crystal cake plate $25.

ENGLISH HOBNAIL

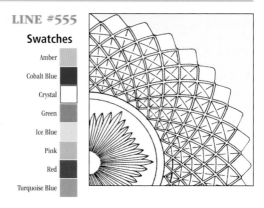

LINE #555

Swatches

Amber
Cobalt Blue
Crystal
Green
Ice Blue
Pink
Red
Turquoise Blue

Manufactured by Westmoreland Glass Company, Grapeville, Pa., from the 1920s to 1983.

Made in amber, cobalt blue, crystal, crystal with various color treatments, green, ice blue, pink, red, and turquoise blue. Values for cobalt blue, red or turquoise blue pieces are about 25 percent higher than ice blue values. Currently, a turquoise basket is valued at $150; a red basket at $100. Crystal pieces with a color accent are slightly higher than crystal values.

Reproductions: † A creamer and sugar with a hexagonal foot have been reproduced, as well as a nut bowl and pickle dish.

Item	Amber	Crystal	Green	Ice Blue	Pink
Ashtray, 3" d	$20	$20	$24	$-	$24
Ashtray, 4-1/2" d	9	9	15	24	15
Ashtray, 4-1/2" sq	9.50	9.50	15	-	15
Basket, 5" d, handle	20	20	-	-	-
Basket, 6" d, handle, tall	40	40	-	-	43
Bonbon, 6-1/2" h, handle	15	17.50	30	40	30
Bowl, 7" d, six parts	17.50	17.50	-	-	-
Bowl, 7" d, oblong spoon	17.50	17.50	-	-	-
Bowl, 8" d, ftd	30	30	48	-	48
Bowl, 8" d, hexagonal foot, two handles	38	38	75	115	75
Bowl, 8", 6 pt	24	24	-	-	-
Bowl, 9-1/2" d, round, crimped	30	30	-	-	-
Bowl, 10" d, flared	35	35	40	-	40
Bowl, 10" l, oval, crimped	40	40	-	-	-
Bowl, 11" d, rolled edge	35	35	40	85	40
Bowl, 12" d, flared	32	32	40	-	95
Bowl,12" l, oval crimped	32	32	-	-	-
Candelabra, two lite	20	20	-	-	-
Candlesticks, pr, 3-1/2" h, round base	24	32	36	-	60
Candlesticks, pr, 5-1/2" h, sq base	30	32	-	-	-
Candlesticks, pr, 9" h, round base	50	40	72	-	125
Candy dish, three feet	45	38	50	-	50
Candy dish, cov, 1/2 lb, cone shape	45	40	55	-	90
Celery, 12" l, oval	24	45	36	-	36

English Hobnail, crystal tumbler $10.

Item	Amber	Crystal	Green	Ice Blue	Pink
Celery, 9" d	18	20	32	-	32
Champagne, two ball, round foot	8	7	20	-	20
Chandelier, 17" shade, 200 prisms	425	400	-	-	-
Cheese, cov, 6" d	40	42	-	-	-
Cheese, cov, 8-3/4" d	50	48	-	-	-
Cigarette box, cov, 4-1/2" x 2-1/2"	24.50	24.50	30	-	55
Cigarette jar, cov, round	16	18	25	-	65
Claret, 5 oz, round	15	17.50	-	-	-
Coaster, 3"	5	5	-	-	-
Cocktail, 3 oz, round	8.50	12	-	-	37.50
Cocktail, 3-1/2 oz, round, ball	15	17.50	-	-	-
Compote, 5" d, round, round foot	22	20	25	-	25
Compote, 5" d, round, sq foot	24	24	-	-	-
Compote, 5-1/2" d, bell	12	15	-	-	-
Compote, 5-1/2" d, bell, sq foot	20	20	-	-	-
Console bowl, 12" d, flange	30	30	40	-	40
Cordial, 1 oz, round, ball	16.50	17.50	-	-	-
Cordial, 1 oz, round, foot	16.50	16.50	-	-	-
Cream soup bowl, 4-5/8" d	15	15	-	-	-
Cream soup liner, round, 6-1/2" d	5	5	-	-	-
Creamer, hexagonal foot †	20	20	25	-	48
Creamer, low, flat	10	10	-	-	-

Item	Amber	Crystal	Green	Ice Blue	Pink
Creamer, sq foot	24	24	45	-	45
Cruet, 12 oz	-	25	-	-	-
Cup	8	12	18	-	25
Decanter, 20 oz	55	55	-	-	-
Demitasse cup	17.50	17.50	55	-	55
Dish, 6" d, crimped	15	15	-	-	-
Egg cup	15	15	-	-	-
Finger bowl, 4-1/2" d	7.50	7.50	15	35	15
Finger bowl, 4-1/2" sq, foot	9.50	9.50	18	40	18
Finger bowl liner, 6" sq	6.50	7	20	-	20
Finger bowl liner, 6-1/2" d, round	12	12	10	-	10
Ginger ale tumbler, 5 oz, flat	10	10	18	-	20
Ginger ale tumbler, 5 oz, round foot	10	10	-	-	-
Ginger ale tumbler, 5 oz, sq foot	8	8	32	-	35
Goblet, 8 oz, 6-1/4" h, round, water	12	12	-	50	35
Goblet, 8 oz, sq foot, water	10	10	-	-	50
Grapefruit bowl, 6-1/2" d	12	12	22	-	24
Hat, high	18	18	-	-	-
Hat, low	15	15	-	-	-
Honey compote, 6" d, round foot	18	18	35	-	35
Honey compote, 6" d, sq foot	18	18	-	-	-
Ice tub, 4" h	18	18	50	-	85
Ice tub, 5-1/2" h	36	36	65	-	100

*English Hobnail, 6" green mayonnaise **$22**, and 8-1/2" green plate **$17.50**.*

Item	Amber	Crystal	Green	Ice Blue	Pink
Iced tea tumbler, 10 oz	14	14	30	-	30
Iced tea tumbler, 11 oz, round, ball	12	12	-	-	-
Iced tea tumbler, 11 oz, sq foot	13.50	13.50	-	-	-
Iced tea tumbler, 12-1/2 oz, round foot	14	24	-	-	-
Iced tea tumbler, 12 oz, flat	14	14	32	-	32
Icer, sq base, patterned insert	45	45	-	-	-
Ivy bowl, 6-1/2" d, sq foot, crimp top	35	45	-	-	-
Juice tumbler, 7 oz, round foot	27.50	27.50	-	-	-
Juice tumbler, 7 oz, sq foot	6.50	6.50	-	-	-
Lamp shade, 17" d	175	165	-	-	-
Lamp, 6-1/2" h, electric	45	45	50	-	50
Lamp, 9-1/2" d, electric	45	45	115	-	115
Lamp, candlestick	32	32	-	-	-
Marmalade, cov	40	40	45	-	70
Mayonnaise, 6"	12	12	22	-	22
Mustard, cov, sq, foot	18	18	-	-	-
Nappy, 4-1/2" d, round	8	8	15	30	15
Nappy, 4-1/2" w, sq	8.50	8.50	-	-	-
Nappy, 5" d, round	10	10	15	35	15
Nappy, 5-1/2" d, bell	12	12	-	-	-
Nappy, 6" d, round	10	10	17.50	-	17.50
Nappy, 6" d, sq	10	10	17.50	-	17.50
Nappy, 6-1/2" d, round	12.50	12.50	20	-	20
Nappy, 6-1/2" d, sq	14	14	-	-	-

Item	Amber	Crystal	Green	Ice Blue	Pink
Nappy, 7" d, round	14	14	24	-	24
Nappy, 7-1/2" d, bell	15	15	-	-	-
Nappy, 8" d, cupped	22	22	30	-	30
Nappy, 8" d, round	22	22	35	-	35
Nappy, 9" d, bell	25	25	-	-	-
Nut, individual, ftd †	6	8	14.50	-	20
Oil bottle, 2 oz, handle	25	25	-	-	-
Oil bottle, 6 oz, handle	27.50	27.50	-	-	-
Old fashioned tumbler, 5 oz	15	15	-	-	-
Oyster cocktail, 5 oz, sq foot	12	12	17.50	-	17.50
Parfait, round foot	17.50	17.50	-	-	-
Pickle, 8" d †	15	15	-	-	-
Pitcher, 23 oz, rounded	48	48	150	-	165
Pitcher, 32 oz, straight side	50	50	175	-	175
Pitcher, 38 oz, rounded	65	65	215	-	215
Pitcher, 60 oz, rounded	70	70	295	-	295
Pitcher, 64 oz, straight side	75	75	310	-	310
Plate, 5-1/2" d, round	7	7	10	-	10
Plate, 6-1/2" d, round	6.25	6.25	10	-	10
Plate, 6-1/2" d, round, depressed center	6	6	-	-	-
Plate, 8" d, round	9	9	14	-	14
Plate, 8" d, round, ftd	13	13	-	-	-
Plate, 8-1/2" d, plain edge	9	9	-	-	-
Plate, 8-1/2" d, round	7	9	17.50	-	28
Plate, 8-3/4" w, sq	9.25	9.25	-	-	-
Plate, 10" d, round	15	15	45	-	65
Plate, 10" w, sq	15	15	-	-	-

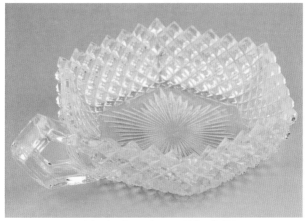

English Hobnail, crystal nappy with handle $22.

Item	Amber	Crystal	Green	Ice Blue	Pink
Plate, 10-1/2" d, round, grill	18	18	-	-	-
Plate, 12" w, sq	20	20	-	-	-
Plate, 15" w, sq	28	28	-	-	-
Preserve, 8" d	15	15	-	-	-
Puff box, cov, 6" d, round	20	20	47.50	-	80
Punch bowl and stand	215	215	-	-	-
Relish, 8" d, three parts	18	18	-	-	-
Rose bowl, 4" d	17.50	17.50	48	-	50
Rose bowl, 6" d	20	20	-	-	-
Salt and pepper shakers, pr, round foot	27.50	27.50	150	-	165
Salt and pepper shakers, pr, sq foot	20	20	-	-	-
Saucer, demitasse, round	10	10	15	-	17.50
Saucer, demitasse, sq	10	10	-	-	-
Saucer, round	2	3	6	-	6
Saucer, sq	2	2	-	-	-
Sherbet, high, round foot	7	10	18	-	37.50
Sherbet, high, sq foot	8	9.50	18	-	-
Sherbet, high, two ball, round foot	10	10	-	-	-
Sherbet, low, one ball, round foot	12	10	-	-	15
Sherbet, low, round foot	12.50	7	-	-	-
Sherbet, low, sq foot	6.50	6	15	-	17.50
Straw jar, 10" h	65	60	-	-	-
Sugar, hexagonal, ftd †	9	9	40	-	48
Sugar, low, flat	8	8	45	-	-
Sugar, sq foot	9	9	48	-	55

Item	Amber	Crystal	Green	Ice Blue	Pink
Sweetmeat, 5-1/2" d, ball stem	30	30	-	-	-
Sweetmeat, 8" d, ball stem	40	40	60	-	65
Tidbit, two tiers	27.50	27.50	65	85	80
Toilet bottle, 5 oz	25	25	40	65	40
Torte plate, 14" d, round	35	30	48	-	48
Torte plate, 20-1/2", round	55	50	-	-	-
Tumbler, 8 oz, water	10	10	24	-	24
Tumbler, 9 oz, round, ftd water	10	10	-	-	-
Tumbler, 9 oz, sq foot, water	10	10	-	-	-
Urn, cov, 11" h	35	35	350	-	350
Vase, 6-1/2" h, sq foot	24	24	-	-	-
Vase, 7-1/2" h, flip	27.50	27.50	70	-	70
Vase, 7-1/2" h, flip jar with cov	55	55	85	-	85
Vase, 8" h, sq foot	35	35	-	-	-
Vase, 8-1/2" h, flared top	40	40	120	-	235
Whiskey, 3 oz	12	15	-	-	-
Wine, 2 oz, round foot	15	12.50	-	-	-
Wine, 2 oz, sq ft	24	24	35	-	65
Wine, 2-1/2 oz, ball, foot	20	20	-	-	-

FAIRFAX

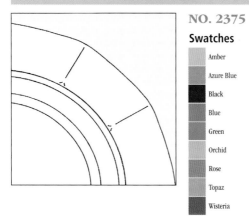

NO. 2375

Swatches

Amber

Azure Blue

Black

Blue

Green

Orchid

Rose

Topaz

Wisteria

Manufactured by Fostoria Glass Company, Moundsville, W. Va., from 1927 to 1944. While this pattern is collected as Fairfax by many, the blanks were also used for some Fostoria etchings, such as June, Trojan, and Versailles. The following values are for the Fairfax pattern; expect to pay more for the etched patterns.

Made in amber, azure blue, black, blue, green, orchid, rose, topaz, and wisteria, with limited production in ruby.

Fairfax, 4-1/4" amber footed sherbet $10, 5" rose footed wine $30, and 8-1/2" blue water goblet $32.

Item	Amber	Azure Blue, Black, and Blue	Green	Orchid, Rose, Wist.	Topaz
After dinner cup and saucer	$15	$30	$18	$30	$18
Ashtray, 2-1/2" d	9	15	12	15	12
Ashtray, 4"	10	17.50	12.50	17.50	12.50
Ashtray, 5-1/2"	12	20	15	20	15
Baker, oval, 9" l	17.50	35	24	35	24
Baker, oval, 10-1/2" l	20	42	25	42	25
Bonbon	10	12.50	12	12.50	12
Bouillon, ftd	8.50	14.50	10	18.50	10
Bowl, 7" d, three ftd	10	15	14	15	14
Bowl, 12" d	22	42	24	42	24
Bread plate, 12" d	27.50	45	30	45	30
Butter dish, cov	80	145	125	145	100
Cake plate, 10" d	15	24	15	24	15
Canapé plate	12	20	15	20	15
Candlesticks, pr, 3" h	25	55	35	37.50	35
Candy, cov, three parts	40	65	67.50	65	50
Candy, cov, ftd	45	70	60	70	60
Celery tray, 11-1/4" l	12	25	17.50	25	17.50
Centerpiece bowl, 12" d	20	40	25	40	25
Centerpiece bowl, 13" l, oval	24	45	35	45	35
Centerpiece bowl, 15" d	27.50	48	37.50	48	40
Cereal bowl, 6" d	12	24	14.50	24	18
Cheese and cracker set	20	45	25	45	25
Chop plate, 13" d	15	25	17.50	25	17.50
Cigarette box	20	48	24	48	24
Claret, 4 oz, 6" h	25	40	35	40	35
Cocktail, 3 oz, 5-1/4" h	12	24	20	24	20

Item	Amber	Azure Blue, Black, and Blue	Green	Orchid, Rose, Wist.	Topaz
Comport, 5"	15	30	20	30	20
Comport, 7"	20	45	27.50	32	27.50
Cordial, 3/4 oz, 4" h	25	65	45	65	45
Cream soup, ftd	10	20	15	20	15
Cream soup underplate	5	8	5	8	5
Creamer, flat	12	-	15	-	15
Creamer, ftd	10	24	12	15	12
Creamer, tea size	9	18.50	12.50	35	12.50
Cup, flat	4.50	-	7.50	-	6.50
Cup, ftd	7.50	15	9	10	9
Dessert bowl, large, handle	15	40	24	40	24
Flower holder, oval	25	85	40	85	40
Fruit bowl, 5" d	8	15	9	15	9
Goblet, 10 oz, 8-1/4" h	17.50	32	22	35	22
Grapefruit	17.50	35	25	35	25
Grapefruit liner	15	32	20	32	22
Ice bowl	12	20	14.50	20	14.50
Ice bowl liner	12	22	12	22	14.50
Ice bucket	32	50	35	50	35
Juice tumbler, 2-1/2 oz, ftd	12	32	18.50	32	18.50
Lemon bowl, two handles, ftd	6.50	12.50	7.50	12.50	7.50
Mayonnaise	10	15	35	20	10
Mayonnaise ladle	20	30	24	30	24
Mayonnaise underplate	5	8	4	8	5
Nappy, 8" d	18	40	24	40	24

Fairfax, topaz bullion soup bowl $10, and footed green cup $9.

Fairfax, 5" amber footed comport $15.

Item	Amber	Azure Blue, Black, and Blue	Green	Orchid, Rose, Wist.	Topaz
Nut cup	15	32	20	32	20
Oil bottle, ftd, os	85	150	110	150	110
Pickle, 8-1/2" l	12	27.50	20	25	15
Pitcher	125	200	155	350	175
Plate, 6" d, bread and butter	2.50	4.50	3	4.50	5
Plate, 7-1/2" d, salad	5	14	4.50	5.50	5
Plate, 8-3/4" d, salad	4.50	12	5.50	7.50	5.50
Plate, 9-1/2" d, luncheon	8	12	7.50	12	7.50
Plate, 10-1/4" d, dinner	18	40	30	40	30
Plate, 10-1/4" d, grill	17.50	40	27.50	40	27.50
Platter, 10-1/2" l	18	35	25	35	25
Platter, 12" l	20	40	32	40	32
Platter, 15" l	30	70	42	70	42
Relish, three parts, 8-1/2" l	12	22	14	22	14
Relish, 11-1/2" l	14	24	17.50	24	17.50
Salad dressing bowl	75	180	90	180	90
Salt and pepper shakers, pr, ftd	35	80	45	60	40
Salt and pepper shakers, pr, individual size	20	-	25	-	25
Sauce boat and underplate	30	65	38	65	40
Saucer	3	6.50	3 .50	5	3.50
Sherbet, 6 oz, 6" h	10	20	12.50	20	12.50
Soup bowl, 7" d	18	40	24	40	24
Sugar bowl, flat	12	-	14	-	14

Item	Amber	Azure Blue, Black, and Blue	Green	Orchid, Rose, Wist.	Topaz
Sugar bowl, ftd	8	24	10	12	10
Sugar bowl, tea size	10	20	14.50	20	14.50
Sugar bowl lid	20	35	25	35	25
Sugar pail	25	60	40	60	40
Sweetmeat	12	17.50	15	17.50	17.50
Tray, 11" d, center handle	15	25	20	25	20
Tumbler, 5 oz, 4-1/2" h, ftd	10	17.50	12	17.50	12
Tumbler, 9 oz, 5-1/4" h, ftd	14.50	20	17.50	20	17.50
Tumbler, 12 oz, 6", ftd	17.50	27.50	25	27.50	25
Vase, 8" h	35	50	35	50	35
Whipped cream pail	25	55	40	40	40
Whipped cream underplate	9	12	10	12	10
Wine, 3 oz, 5-1/2" h	20	30	25	30	30

FLORAGOLD

LOUISA

Swatches

Crystal

Ice Blue

Iridescent

Shell Pink

Manufactured by Jeannette Glass Company, Jeannette, Pa., 1950s.

Made in iridescent. Some large comports were later made in ice blue, crystal, red-yellow, and shell pink.

Item	Iridescent
Ashtray, 4" d	**$7**
Bowl, 4-1/2" sq	5
Bowl, 5-1/4" d, ruffled	15
Bowl, 8-1/2" d, sq	20
Bowl, 8-1/2" d, ruffled	10
Butter dish, cov, 1/4 pound, oblong	30
Butter dish, cov, round, 5-1/2" w sq base	800
Butter dish, cov, round, 6-1/4" w sq base	55
Candlesticks, pr, double branch	60
Candy dish, one handle	12.50

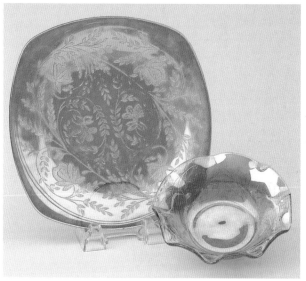

Floragold, 5-1/4" d iridescent dinner plate $40 and ruffled berry bowl $15.

Item	Iridescent
Candy or cheese dish, cov, 6-3/4" d	130
Candy, 5-3/4" l, four feet	12
Celery vase	420
Cereal bowl, 5-1/2" d, round	40
Coaster, 4" d	10
Comport, 5-1/4", plain top	750
Comport, 5-1/4", ruffled top	850
Creamer	15
Cup	8
Fruit bowl, 5-1/2" d, ruffled	8.50
Fruit bowl, 12" d, ruffled, large	12
Nappy, 5" d, one handle	12
Pitcher, 64 oz	55
Plate, 5-1/4" d, sherbet	12
Plate, 8-1/2" d, dinner	48
Platter, 11-1/4" d	28
Salad bowl, 9-1/2" d, deep	50
Salt and pepper shakers, pr, plastic tops	60
Saucer, 5-1/4" d	15
Sherbet, low, ftd	15
Sugar	15
Sugar lid	15
Tidbit, wooden post	35
Tray, 13-1/2" d	50
Tray, 13-1/2" d, with indent	65
Tumbler, 11 oz, ftd	20
Tumbler, 10 oz, ftd	20
Tumbler, 15 oz, ftd	110
Vase	420

FLORAL

POINSETTIA

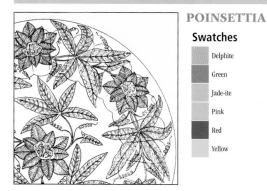

Swatches

	Delphite
	Green
	Jade-ite
	Pink
	Red
	Yellow

Manufactured by Jeannette Glass Company, Jeannette, Pa., from 1931 to 1935.

Made in amber, crystal, Delphite, green, Jad-ite, pink, red, and yellow. Production in amber, crystal, red, and yellow was limited. A crystal 6-7/8" h vase is valued at $295.

Reproductions: † Reproduction salt and pepper shakers have been made in cobalt blue, dark green, green, pink, and red.

Item	Delphite	Green	Jade-ite	Pink
Berry bowl, 4" d	$50	$25	$-	$25
Butter dish, cov	-	95	-	100
Candlesticks, pr, 4" h	-	90	-	95
Candy jar, cov	80	50	-	48
Canister set	-	-	60	-
Casserole, cov	-	45	-	28

Floral, pink dinner plate $27.50.

Item	Delphite	Green	Jad-ite	Pink
Coaster, 3-1/4" d	-	15 .50	-	12.50
Comport, 9"	-	875	-	795
Cream soup, 5-1/2" d	-	735	-	735
Creamer, flat	-	18	-	25
Cup	-	15	-	15
Dresser set	-	1,350	-	-
Dresser tray, 9-1/4" l, oval	-	200	-	-
Flower frog	-	695	-	-
Ice tub, 3-1/2" h, oval	-	850	-	825
Juice tumbler, ftd	-	20	-	22
Juice tumbler, 5 oz, 4" h, flat	-	35	-	35
Lamp	-	295	-	260
Lemonade pitcher, 48 oz, 10-1/4" h	-	295	-	350
Lemonade tumbler, 9 oz, 5-1/4" h, ftd	-	60	-	60
Pitcher, 23 or 24 oz, 5-1/2" h	-	595	-	45
Pitcher, 32 oz, ftd, cone, 8" h	-	45	-	60
Plate, 6" d, sherbet	-	12	-	10
Plate, 8" d, salad	-	15	-	20
Plate, 9" d, dinner	145	30	-	27.50
Plate, 9" d, grill	-	185	-	-
Plate, 10-3/4" l, oval	-	20	-	17.50
Platter, 11" l	150	25	-	24
Refrigerator dish, cov, 5" sq	-	-	15	-
Relish, two parts, oval	165	32	-	32
Rose bowl, three legs	-	500	-	-
Salad bowl, 7-1/2" d	-	40	-	40
Salad bowl, 7-1/2" d, ruffled	65	125	-	120
Salt and pepper shakers, pr, 4" h, ftd †	-	60	-	50
Salt and pepper shakers, pr, 6" flat	-	-	-	60

Item	Delphite	Green	Jad-ite	Pink
Saucer	-	12.50	-	12.50
Sherbet	90	30	-	20
Sugar, cov	-	32	-	30
Sugar, open	75	-	-	-
Tray, 6" sq, closed handles	-	195	-	-
Tumbler, 3 oz, 3-1/2" h, ftd	-	18	-	25
Tumbler, 7 oz, 4-1/2", ftd	175	25	-	22
Tumbler, 5-1/4" h, ftd	-	60	-	55
Vase, flared, three legs	-	485	-	-
Vase, 6-7/8" h	-	475	-	-
Vegetable bowl, 8" d, cov	-	50	-	65
Vegetable bowl, 8" d, open	80	-	-	40
Vegetable bowl, 9" l, oval	-	35	-	40

Floral, green berry bowl $25, and green sherbet $30.

FLORAL AND DIAMOND BAND

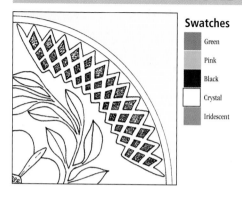

Swatches

- Green
- Pink
- Black
- Crystal
- Iridescent

Manufactured by U.S. Glass Company, Pittsburgh, Pa., in the late 1920s.

Made in pink and green with limited production in black, crystal, and iridescent.

Item	Green	Pink
Berry bowl, 4-1/2" d	$12	$15
Berry bowl, 8" d	15	18
Butter dish, cov	140	150
Compote, 5-1/2" h	18	17.50
Creamer, 4-3/4"	20	17.50
Iced tea tumbler, 5" h	45	65
Nappy, 5-3/4" d, handle	12	11
Pitcher, 42 oz, 8" h	95	90
Plate, 8" d, luncheon	55	45
Sherbet	10	9.50

Item	Green	Pink
Sugar, cov, 5-1/4"	70	55
Tumbler, 4" h, water	25	25

Floral and Diamond Band, green luncheon plate $55.

FLORENTINE NO. 1

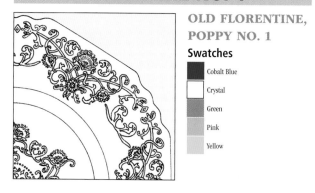

OLD FLORENTINE, POPPY NO. 1

Swatches

Cobalt Blue

Crystal

Green

Pink

Yellow

Manufactured by Hazel Atlas Glass Company, Clarksburg, W.V., and Zanesville, Ohio, from 1932 to 1935.

Made in crystal, green, pink, yellow, and limited production in cobalt blue.

Reproductions: † Salt and pepper shakers have been reproduced in cobalt blue, pink, and red.

Item	Cobalt Blue	Crystal	Green	Pink	Yellow
Ashtray, 5-1/2" d	$-	$24	$24	$28	$28
Berry bowl, 5" d	24	15	40	40	15
Berry bowl, 8-1/2" d	-	24	25	28	28
Butter dish, cov	-	110	140	165	160
Cereal bowl, 6" d	-	32	32	35	35
Coaster/ashtray, 3-3/4" d	-	18	20	25	25
Comport, 3-1/2" h, ruffled	60	25	25	15	-

Item	Cobalt Blue	Crystal	Green	Pink	Yellow
Cream soup, 5" d, ruffled	50	15	18	20	-
Creamer	-	9	15	20	20
Creamer, ruffled	65	45	35	37	-
Cup	85	5	10	18	13.50
Iced tea tumbler, 12 oz, 5-1/4" h, ftd	-	28	28	30	24
Juice tumbler, 5 oz, 3-3/4" h, ftd	-	16	16	20	22
Lemonade tumbler, 9 oz, 5-1/4" h	-	-	-	100	-
Pitcher, 36 oz, 6-1/2", ftd	850	45	45	65	50
Pitcher, 48 oz, 7-1/2", flat, with or without ice lip	-	75	75	135	195
Plate, 6" d, sherbet	-	7.50	9	7.50	9
Plate, 8-1/2" d, salad	-	9	12.50	14	14.50
Plate, 10" d, dinner	-	16	20	22	24
Plate, 10" d, grill	-	12	12.50	20	22
Platter, 11-1/2" l, oval	-	19	10	22	35
Salt and pepper shakers, pr, ftd †	-	22	60	55	60
Saucer	18	3	4.50	6	3
Sherbet, 3 oz, ftd	-	8	10	15	14
Sugar, cov	-	10	12.50	25	12
Sugar, ruffled	55	35	30	42.50	-
Tumbler, 4 oz, 3-1/4" h, ftd	-	15	16	-	-
Tumbler, 9 oz, 4" h, ribbed	-	12	14	22	-
Tumbler, 10 oz, 4-3/4" h, ftd	-	22	20	22	24
Vegetable bowl, cov, 9-1/2" l, oval	-	45	45	60	60

Florentine No. 1, green creamer $15, and covered sugar $12.50.

Florentine #1, 8-1/2" pink berry bowl $28.

FLORENTINE NO. 2

Swatches

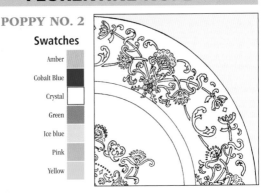

Amber

Cobalt Blue

Crystal

Green

Ice blue

Pink

Yellow

Manufactured by Hazel Atlas Glass Company, Clarksburg, W.V., and Zanesville, Ohio, from 1932 to 1935.

Made in amber, cobalt blue, crystal, green, ice blue, pink, and yellow. Ice blue production is limited to 7-1/2" h pitcher, valued at $525. Amber production is limited to 9 oz and 12 oz tumblers, both currently valued at $80; cup and saucer, valued at $75; and sherbet, valued at $45. Cobalt blue production is limited to 3-1/2" comport, valued at $60, and 9 oz tumbler, valued at $80.

Reproductions: † 7-1/2" h cone-shaped pitcher and 4" h footed tumbler. Reproductions are found in amber, cobalt blue, crystal, deep green, and pink.

Item	Crystal	Green	Pink	Yellow
Ashtray, 3-1/2" d	$18.50	$18.50	$-	$25
Ashtray, 5-1/2" d	20	25	-	32

Item	Crystal	Green	Pink	Yellow
Berry bowl, 4-1/2" d	12.50	16.50	17.50	27.50
Berry bowl, 8" d	24	26	30	35
Bowl, 5-1/2" d	32	35	-	42
Bowl, 7-1/2" d, shallow	-	-	-	85
Bowl, 9" d, flat	27.50	27.50	-	-
Butter dish, cov	115	125	-	165
Candlesticks, pr, 2-3/4" h	45	48	-	70
Candy dish, cov	120	115	150	170
Cereal bowl, 6" d	28	28	-	40
Coaster, 3-1/4" d	-	-	-	25
Coaster, 3-3/4" d	18.50	18.50	-	25
Coaster, 5-1/2" d	20	25	-	35
Cocktail, 3-1/4" h, ftd	-	-	-	14.50
Comport, 3-1/2" d, ruffled	25	25	25	-
Condiment tray, round	-	-	-	65
Cream soup, 4-3/4" d, two handles	12.50	16	18.50	20
Creamer	5	12	-	14.50
Cup	5.50	10	-	12
Custard cup	60	60	-	140
Gravy boat	-	-	-	65
Gravy boat underplate, 11-1/2" l	-	-	-	95
Iced tea tumbler, 12 oz, 5" h	35	35	-	45
Juice tumbler, 5 oz, 3-1/8" h, flat	14.50	14.50	16	22
Juice tumbler, 5 oz, 3-1/8" h, ftd	13	15	-	22
Parfait, 6" h	30	32	-	65
Pitcher, 28 oz, ftd, 7-1/2" h †	60	40	-	50
Pitcher, 48 oz, 7-1/2" h	60	70	120	32
Pitcher, 76 oz, 8-1/4" h	90	95	225	400
Plate, 6" d, sherbet	6	6	-	9.50

Item	Crystal	Green	Pink	Yellow
Plate, 6-1/2" d, indent	16	17.50	-	30
Plate, 8-1/2" d, salad	8.50	9.50	9	10
Plate, 10" d, dinner	16.50	16	-	15
Plate, 10-1/4" d, grill	15	15	-	18.50
Plate, 10-1/4" d, grill, cream soup ring	35	35	-	-
Platter, 11" oval	15	20	18.50	25
Relish, 10" d, divided, three parts	22.50	24	26	35
Relish, 10" d, plain	22.50	24	26	32

Florentine No. 2, yellow cup **$12.**

REPRODUCTION! Florentine No. 2, green pitcher and tumbler.

Item	Crystal	Green	Pink	Yellow
Salt and pepper shakers, pr	48	50	-	60
Saucer	5	6	-	5
Sherbet, ftd	10	12.50	-	12.50
Sugar, cov	6.50	9	-	38
Tumbler, 5 oz, 3-1/4" h, ftd	18	15	15	-
Tumbler, 5 oz, 4" h, ftd †	13.50	15	18	20
Tumbler, 5 oz, 3-5/16" h, blown	18.50	18.50	-	-
Tumbler, 6 oz, 3-9/16" h, blown	16	18.50	-	-
Tumbler, 9 oz, 4" h	12.50	18.50	16	22.50
Tumbler, 9 oz, 4-1/2" h, ftd	25	25	-	38
Tumbler, 10 oz, 4-11/16" h, blown	19	19	-	-
Tumbler, 12 oz, 5" h, blown	20	20	-	20
Vase, 6" h	30	32	-	65
Vegetable bowl, cov, 9" l, oval	55	60	-	85

Florentine #2, 8" green berry bowl $26.

FLOWER GARDEN WITH BUTTERFLIES

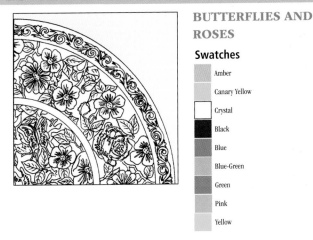

BUTTERFLIES AND ROSES

Swatches

Amber

Canary Yellow

Crystal

Black

Blue

Blue-Green

Green

Pink

Yellow

Manufactured by U.S. Glass Company, Pittsburgh, Pa., in the late 1920s.

Made in amber, black, blue, blue-green, canary yellow, crystal, green, and pink.

Item	Amber or Crystal	Black	Blue-Green, Green or Pink	Blue or Canary Yellow
Ashtray	$175	$-	$185	$225
Bonbon, cov, 6-5/8" d	-	265	-	-
Bowl, 9" d, rolled edge	-	225	-	-
Candlesticks, pr, 4" h	50	-	60	100

Item	Amber or Crystal	Black	Blue-Green, Green or Pink	Blue or Canary Yellow
Candlesticks, pr, 8" h	90	325	145	145
Candy, cov, 6" d, flat	135	-	165	-
Candy, cov, 7-1/2" cone shape	90	100	165	175
Candy, cov, heart shape	-	-	1,250	1,500
Cologne bottle, 7-1/2" h	-	-	225	365
Comport, 2-7/8" h	-	250	40	45
Comport, 3" h	25	-	30	35
Comport, 4-1/4" h, 4-3/4" w	-	-	-	65

Flower Garden with Butterflies, blue comport $90.

Item	Amber or Crystal	Black	Blue-Green, Green or Pink	Blue or Canary Yellow
Comport, 4-3/4" h, 10-1/4" w	50	250	70	90
Comport, 5-7/8" h, 11" w	60	-	-	95
Comport, 7-1/4" h, 8-1/4" w	65	175	85	-
Creamer	-	-	75	-
Cup	-	-	70	-
Orange bowl, 11" d, ftd	-	250	-	-
Plate, 7" d	20	-	25	30
Plate, 8" d	17.50	-	20	27.50
Plate, 10" d	-	-	45	50
Plate, 10" d, indent	35	150	45	50
Powder jar, 3-1/2", flat	-	-	75	-
Powder jar, 6-1/4" h, ftd	225	-	130	175
Powder jar, 7-1/2" h, ftd	85	-	135	195
Sandwich server, center handle	55	135	75	100
Saucer	-	-	30	-
Tray, 5-1/2" x 10", oval	50	-	75	9
Tray, 11-3/4" x 7-3/4", rect	50	-	75	90
Tumbler, 7-1/2 oz	175	-	-	-
Vase, 6-1/4" h	75	145	135	145
Vase, 8" h, Dahlia, cupped	-	275	-	-
Vase, 10" h, two handles	-	250	-	-
Vase, 10-1/2" h	-	-	150	225
Wall pocket, 9" l	-	365	-	-

FOREST GREEN

Swatches

Forest Green

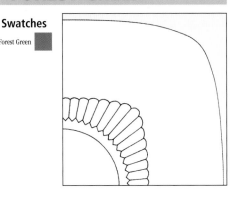

Manufactured by Anchor Hocking Glass Company, Lancaster, Ohio, and Long Island City, N.Y., from 1950 to 1957.

Made only in forest green.

Item	Forest Green
Ashtray, 3-1/2" sq	$5
Ashtray, 4-5/8" sq	6
Ashtray, 5-3/4" hexagon	8
Ashtray, 5-3/4" sq	7.50
Batter bowl, spout	25
Berry bowl, large	15
Berry bowl, small	7.50
Bonbon, 6-1/4" w, tricorn	12
Bowl, 4-1/2" w, sq	7
Bowl, 5-1/4" deep	10
Bowl, 6" w, sq	18

Item	Forest Green
Bowl, 6-1/2" d, scalloped	10
Bowl, 6-3/8" d, three toes	15
Bowl, 7-3/8" w, sq	30
Bowl, 7-1/2" d, crimped	10
Cocktail, 3-1/2 oz	12
Cocktail, 4-1/2 oz	14
Creamer, flat	7.50
Cup, sq	7
Dessert bowl, 4-3/4" d	7
Goblet, 9 oz	10
Goblet, 9-1/2 oz	14
Iced tea tumbler, 13 oz	8
Iced tea tumbler, 14 oz, Boopie	8
Iced tea tumbler, 15 oz, tall	10
Iced tea tumbler, 32 oz, giant	18
Ivy ball, 4" h	5
Juice roly-poly tumbler, 3-3/8" h	6
Juice tumbler, 4 oz	10
Juice tumbler, 5-1/2 oz	12.50
Ladle, all green glass	80
Mixing bowl, 6" d	12
Pitcher, 22 oz	22.50
Pitcher, 36 oz	25
Pitcher, 86 oz, round	45
Plate, 6-3/4" d, salad	7.50
Plate, 7" w, sq	6.75
Plate, 8-3/8" d, luncheon	9
Plate, 9-1/4" d, dinner	33.50
Platter, 11" l, rect	22
Popcorn bowl, 5-1/4" d	10

Item	Forest Green
Punch bowl	25
Punch bowl and stand	60
Punch cup	3
Relish tray, 4-3/4" x 6-3/4" l, two handles	25
Roly-poly tumbler, 5 1/8" h	7.50
Salad bowl, 7-3/8" d	15
Sandwich plate, 13-3/4" d	45
Saucer, 5-3/8" w	3
Sherbet, 6 oz	9
Sherbet, 6 oz, Boopie	7
Sherbet, flat	7.50
Soup bowl, 6" d	17
Sugar, flat	7
Tray, 6" x 10", two handles	30

Forest Green, cup $7, and saucer $3.

Item	Forest Green
Tumbler, 5 oz, 3-1/2" h	4
Tumbler, 7 oz	4.50
Tumbler, 5-1/4" h	7
Tumbler, 9-1/2 oz, tall	8
Tumbler, 9 oz, fancy	7
Tumbler, 9 oz, table	5
Tumbler, 10 oz, 4-1/2" h, ftd	8.50
Tumbler, 11 oz	7
Tumbler, 14 oz, 5" h	8
Tumbler, 15 oz, long boy	10
Vase, 6-3/8" h, Harding	7.50
Vase, 7" h, crimped	15
Vase, 9" h	22
Vegetable bowl, 8-1/2" l, oval	30

Forest Green, 4-1/2" bowl $7.

FORTUNE

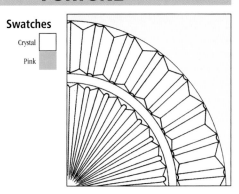

Swatches

Crystal

Pink

Manufactured by Hocking Glass Company, Lancaster, Ohio, from 1937 to 1938.

Made in crystal and pink.

Item	Crystal	Pink
Berry bowl, 4" d	**$10**	**$12**
Berry bowl, 7-3/4" d	25	28
Bowl, 4-1/2" d, handle	12	15
Bowl, 5-1/4" d, rolled edge	20	22
Candy dish, cov, flat	28	30
Cup	12	15
Dessert bowl, 4-1/2" d	12	12
Juice tumbler, 5 oz, 3-1/2" h	12	13.50
Plate, 6" d, sherbet	8	15

Item	Crystal	Pink
Plate, 8" d, luncheon	25	25
Salad bowl, 7-3/4" d	25	25
Saucer	5	8.50
Tumbler, 9 oz, 4" h	15	16.50

Fortune, 6" pink plate $15, 4" pink berry bowl $12, and 4-1/2" pink bowl with one handle $15.

FRUITS

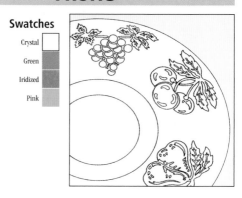

Swatches

Crystal

Green

Iridized

Pink

Manufactured by Hazel Atlas Company, and several other small glass companies, from 1931 to 1935.

Made in crystal, green, iridized, and pink. Iridized production includes only a 4" tumbler, valued at $10.

Item	Crystal	Green	Pink
Berry bowl, 5" d	$17.50	$32	$28
Berry bowl, 8" d	40	85	45
Cup	5	12	7
Juice tumbler, 5 oz, 3-1/2" h	20	60	22
Pitcher, 7" h	50	95	-
Plate, 8" d, luncheon	12	15	12
Saucer	2.50	6	4.50
Sherbet	10	15	12
Tumbler, 4" h, multiple fruits	15	24	22

Item	Crystal	Green	Pink
Tumbler, 4" h, single fruit	20	30	25
Tumbler, 12 oz, 5" h	70	200	95

Fruits, green cup $12, and saucer $6.

GEORGIAN

Swatches

Crystal

Green

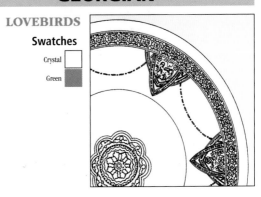

Manufactured by Federal Glass Company, Columbus, Ohio, from 1931 to 1936.

Made in green. A crystal hot plate is valued at $25.

Item	Green
Berry bowl, 4-1/2" d	**$15**
Berry bowl, 7-1/2" d, large	**65**
Bowl, 6-1/2" d, deep	**65**
Butter dish, cov	**85**
Cereal bowl, 5-3/4" d	**28.50**
Cold cuts server, 18-1/2" d, wood, seven openings for 5" d coasters	**875**
Creamer, 3" d, ftd	**40**
Creamer, 4" d, ftd	**20**
Cup	**10**
Hot plate, 5" d, center design	**48**
Plate, 6" d, sherbet	**7.50**

Georgian, 4" green sugar $35, and creamer $20.

Georgian, 4-1/2" green berry bowl $15, and 6" green plate $7.50.

Item	Green
Plate, 8" d, luncheon	12
Plate, 9-1/4" d, center design only	25
Plate, 9-1/4" d, dinner	36
Platter, 11-1/2" l, closed handle	70
Saucer	4
Sherbet, ftd	16
Sugar cover, 3" d	15
Sugar cover, 4" d	15
Sugar, 3" d, ftd	35
Sugar, 4" d, ftd	35
Tumbler, 9 oz, 4" h, flat	65
Tumbler 12 oz, 5-1/4" h, flat	125
Vegetable bowl, 9" l, oval	65

*Georgian, green
sherbet $16.*

HARP

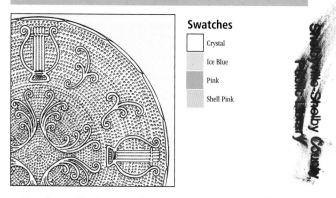

Manufactured by Jeannette Glass Company, Jeannette, Pa., from 1954 to 1957.

Made in crystal and crystal with gold trim; limited pieces made in ice blue, pink, and shell pink.

Swatches

- Crystal
- Ice Blue
- Pink
- Shell Pink

Item	Crystal	Ice Blue	Shell Pink
Ashtray	$10	$-	$-
Cake stand, 9" d	35	45	50
Coaster	6	-	-
Cup	30	-	-
Parfait	20	-	-
Plate, 7" d	25	25	-
Saucer	14	-	-
Snack set, cup, saucer, 7" plate	48	-	-
Tray, two handles, rectangular	35	35	65
Vase, 7-1/2" h	30	-	-

Harp, crystal with gold trim, 7" plate $25 and cake stand $35.

HERITAGE

Swatches

■	Blue
□	Crystal
■	Green
■	Pink

Manufactured by Federal Glass Company, Columbus, Ohio, from 1940 to 1955.

Made in blue, crystal, green, and pink.

Reproductions: † Bowls have been reproduced in amber, crystal, and green. Some are marked with N or MC.

Item	Blue	Crystal	Green	Pink
Berry bowl, 5" d †	$80	$8	$75	$75
Berry bowl, 8-1/2" d †	250	40	200	195
Creamer, ftd	-	25	-	-
Cup	-	7.50	-	-
Fruit bowl, 10-1/2" d	-	15	-	-
Plate, 9-1/4" d, dinner	-	12	-	-
Sandwich plate, 12" d	-	18	-	-
Saucer	-	4	-	-
Sugar, open, ftd	-	25	-	-

Heritage, 9-1/4" d, crystal plate $12.

HEX OPTIC

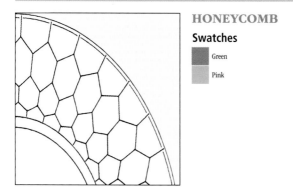

HONEYCOMB

Swatches

Green

Pink

Manufactured by Jeannette Glass Company, Jeannette, Pa., from 1928 to 1932.

Made in green and pink. Ultramarine tumblers have been found.

Item	Green	Pink
Berry bowl, 4-1/4" d, ruffled	**$9.50**	**$8.50**
Berry bowl, 7-1/2" d	15	12
Bucket reamer	65	60
Butter dish, cov, rect, 1-lb size	90	90
Creamer, two style handles	8	7
Cup, two style handles	5	5
Ice bucket, metal handle	30	30
Mixing bowl, 8-1/4" d	18	18
Mixing bowl, 9" d	20	20

Hex Optic, green salt shaker $15, and green sherbet $5.

Hex Optic, green luncheon plate $6, and bucket reamer base $45.

Item	Green	Pink
Mixing bowl, 10" d	20	20
Pitcher, 32 oz, 5" h	25	25
Pitcher, 48 oz, 9" h, ftd	48	50
Pitcher, 96 oz, 8" h	225	235
Plate, 6" d, sherbet	3	3
Plate, 8" d, luncheon	6	6
Platter, 11" d, round	14	16
Refrigerator dish, 4" x 4"	20	18
Refrigerator stack set, 4 pcs	75	75
Salt and pepper shakers, pr	30	30
Saucer	4	4
Sherbet, 5 oz, ftd	5	5
Sugar, two styles of handles	6	6
Sugar shaker	225	225
Tumbler, 12 oz, 5" h	8	8
Tumbler, 5-3/4" h, ftd	10	10
Tumbler, 7" h, ftd	15	12
Tumbler, 7 oz, 4-3/4" h, ftd	8	8
Tumbler, 9 oz, 3-3/4" h	5	5
Whiskey, 1 oz, 2" h	8.50	8.50

HOBNAIL

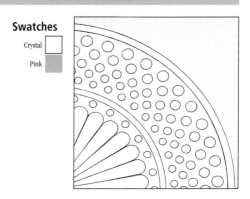

Manufactured by Hocking Glass Company, Lancaster, Ohio, from 1934 to 1936.

Made in crystal, crystal with red trim, and pink.

Item	Crystal	Crystal, red trim	Pink
Cereal bowl, 5-1/2" d	$4.25	$4.25	$-
Cordial, 5 oz, ftd	6	6	-
Creamer, ftd	10	4	-
Cup	5	5	10
Decanter and stopper, 32 oz	27.50	60	-
Goblet, 10 oz	7.50	7.50	-
Iced tea goblet, 13 oz	8.50	8.50	-
Iced tea tumbler, 15 oz	8.50	8.50	-
Juice tumbler, 5 oz	4	4	-

Item	Crystal	Crystal, red trim	Pink
Milk pitcher, 18 oz	32.50	32	-
Pitcher, 67 oz	25	25	-
Plate, 6" d, sherbet	2.50	2.50	7.50
Plate, 8-1/2" d, luncheon	5	5	7.50
Salad bowl, 7" d	5	5	-
Saucer	4	4	6
Sherbet	4	4	10
Sugar, ftd	10	8	-
Tumbler, 9 oz, 4-3/4" h, flat	5	5	-
Whiskey, 1-1/2 oz	5	5	-
Wine, 3 oz, ftd	6.50	6.50	-

Hobnail, pink sherbet $6.

HOLIDAY

BUTTON AND BOWS

Swatches

Crystal	(white)
Iridescent	(gray)
Pink	(pink)
Shell Pink	(hatched)

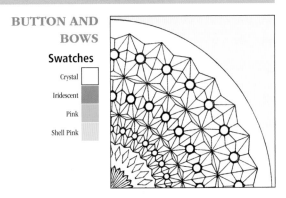

Manufactured by Jeannette Glass Company, Jeannette, Pa., from 1947 to the 1950s.

Made in crystal, iridescent, pink, and shell pink. Shell pink production was limited to the console bowl, valued at $48.

Item	Crystal	Irid.	Pink
Berry bowl, 5-1/8" d	$-	$-	$18
Berry bowl, 8-1/2" d	-	-	55
Butter dish, cov	-	-	75
Cake plate, 10-1/2" d, three legs	-	-	150
Candlesticks, pr, 3" h	-	-	150
Chop plate, 13-3/4" d	-	-	140
Console bowl, 10-1/4" d	-	-	225
Creamer, ftd	-	-	18
Cup, plain	-	-	10
Cup, rayed bottom, 2" d base	-	-	10

Holiday, 9-1/2" pink oval vegetable bowl $36.

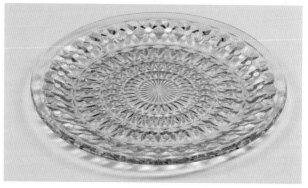

Holiday, 9" pink dinner plate $25.

Item	Crystal	Irid.	Pink
Cup, rayed bottom, 2-3/8" d base	-	-	16
Juice tumbler, 5 oz, 4" h, ftd	-	-	60
Pitcher, 16 oz, 4-3/4" h	17.50	35	85
Pitcher, 52 oz, 6-3/4" h	-	-	45
Plate, 6" d, sherbet	-	-	10
Plate, 9" d, dinner	-	-	25
Platter, 11-3/8" l, oval	-	17.50	35
Sandwich tray, 10-1/2" l	-	20	28
Saucer, plain center	-	-	5
Saucer, rayed center, 2-1/8" d ring	-	-	7.50
Saucer, rayed center, 2-1/2" d ring	-	-	7.50
Sherbet	-	-	10
Soup bowl, 7-3/4" d	-	-	65
Sugar, cov	-	-	12
Sugar lid	-	-	20
Tumbler, 5 oz, 4" h, ftd	-	15	35
Tumbler, 5-1/4 oz, 4-1/4" h, ftd	8	-	45
Tumbler, 6" h, ftd	-	-	195
Tumbler, 9 oz, 4" h, ftd	-	-	55
Tumbler, 10 oz, 4" h, flat	-	-	25
Vegetable bowl, 9-1/2" l, oval	-	-	36

Holiday, 4-3/4" h pink pitcher $85.

HOMESPUN

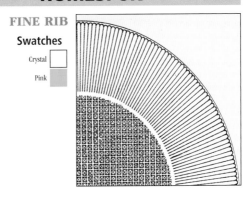

FINE RIB

Swatches

Crystal

Pink

Manufactured by Jeannette Glass Company, Jeannette, Pa., from 1939 to 1949.

Made in crystal and pink.

Item	Crystal	Pink
Ashtray	$6	$6
Berry bowl, 4-1/2" d, closed handles	15	20
Berry bowl, 8-1/4" d	20	20
Butter dish, cov	55	90
Cereal bowl, 5" d, closed handles	30	30
Coaster	6	6
Creamer, ftd	12.50	12.50
Cup	12	15
Iced tea tumbler, 13 oz, 5-1/4" h	32	32
Plate, 6" d, sherbet	7.50	12.50
Plate, 9-1/4" d, dinner	18	18

Item	Crystal	Pink
Platter, 13" d, closed handles	20	20
Saucer	5.50	10
Sherbet, low, flat	17.50	19
Sugar, ftd	12.50	12.50
Tumbler, 5 oz, 4" h, ftd	8	10
Tumbler, 6 oz, 3-7/8" h, straight	7	7.50
Tumbler, 9 oz, 4" h, flared top	17.50	17.50
Tumbler, 9 oz, 4-1/4" h, top band	17.50	17.50
Tumbler, 15 oz, 6-1/4" h, ftd	38	38
Tumbler, 15 oz, 6-3/8" h, ftd	36	36

Children's

Item	Crystal	Pink
Cup	$25	$35
Plate	10	185
Saucer	9	12
Teapot	-	125

Homespun, pink sugar $12.50, and look-alike tumbler.

Homespun, 9-1/4" pink dinner plate $18.

HORSESHOE

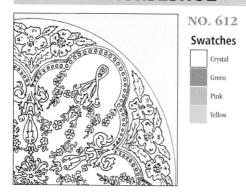

NO. 612

Swatches

☐	Crystal
☐	Green
☐	Pink
☐	Yellow

Manufactured by Indiana Glass Company, Dunkirk, Ind., from 1930 to 1933.

Made in crystal, green, pink, and yellow. There is limited collector interest in crystal and pink at the current time.

Item	Green	Yellow
Berry bowl, 4-1/2" d	$30	$25
Berry bowl, 9-1/2" d	40	35
Butter dish, cov	995	-
Candy dish, metal holder	175	-
Cereal bowl, 6-1/2" d	50	35
Creamer, ftd	30	30
Cup and saucer	20	28
Pitcher, 64 oz, 8-1/2" h	295	350
Plate, 6" d, sherbet	9	10
Plate, 8-3/8" d, salad	10	18

Item	Green	Yellow
Plate, 9-3/8" d, luncheon	15	20
Plate, 10-3/8" d, grill	175	165
Platter, 10-3/4" l, oval	25	25
Relish, three parts, ftd	40	42.50
Salad bowl, 7-1/2" d	24	24
Sandwich plate, 11-1/2" d	24	27.50
Saucer	10	10
Sherbet	16	18.50
Sugar, open	25	27.50
Tumbler, 9 oz, ftd	25	30
Tumbler, 9 oz, 4-1/4" h	150	-

Horseshoe, yellow cup $17.50.

Item	Green	Yellow
Tumbler, 12 oz, ftd	140	150
Tumbler, 12 oz, 4-3/4" h	150	-
Vegetable bowl, 8-1/2" d	30	30
Vegetable bowl, 10-1/2" d, oval	25	50

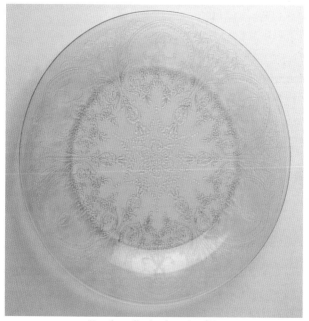

Horseshoe, yellow luncheon plate $20.

INDIANA CUSTARD

FLOWER AND LEAF BAND

Swatches

French Ivory

Manufactured by Indiana Glass Company, Dunkirk, Ind., in the 1930s and in the 1950s.

Made in custard color, known as French Ivory.

Item	French Ivory
Berry bowl, 5-1/2" d	$20
Berry bowl, 9" d, 1-3/4" deep	36
Butter dish, cov	70
Cereal bowl, 6-1/2" d	32
Creamer	22
Cup	38
Plate, 5-3/4" d, bread and butter	7.50
Plate, 7-1/2" d, salad	16
Plate, 8-7/8" d, luncheon	18
Plate, 9-3/4" d, dinner	28
Platter, 11-1/2" l, oval	30

Item	French Ivory
Saucer	8
Sherbet	90
Soup bowl, 7-1/2" d, flat	32
Sugar, cov	35

Indiana Custard, covered sugar $35.

IRIS

IRIS AND HERRINGBONE

Swatches

Crystal

Iridescent

Green

Pink

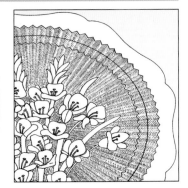

Manufactured by Jeannette Glass Company, Jeannette, Pa., from 1928 to 1932 and in the 1950s and 1970s.

Made in crystal, iridescent, some green, and pink. Recent color combinations of red with yellow, blue with green, and white have been made.

Reproductions: † Some collectors and dealers feel strongly that the newer re-issues of this pattern are actually reproductions. Forms that have the potential to fool buyers are the 4-1/2" berry bowl, covered candy jar, 10" d dinner plate, 6-1/2" h footed tumbler, and vase. Careful examination of the object, plus careful consideration of the color, should help determine age.

Item	Crystal	Green	Iridescent	Pink
Berry bowl, 4-1/2" d, beaded edge †	$60	$-	$32	$-
Berry bowl, 8" d, beaded edge	125	-	30	-
Bowl, 5-1/2" d, scalloped	12	-	25	-
Bowl, 9-1/2" d, scalloped	20	-	15	-
Bread plate, 11-3/4" d	20	-	38	-
Butter dish, cov	60	-	65	-
Candlesticks, pr	50	-	50	-
Candy jar, cov †	235	-	-	-
Cereal bowl, 5" d	140	-	-	-
Coaster †	115	-	-	-
Cocktail, 4 oz, 4-1/4" h	25	-	-	-
Creamer, ftd	12	135	15	150
Cup	20	-	18	-
Demitasse cup and saucer	225	-	350	-
Fruit bowl, 11" d, straight edge	70	-	-	-
Fruit bowl, 11-1/2" d, ruffled	20	-	25	-
Fruit set	75	-	-	-
Goblet, 4 oz, 5-3/4" h	30	-	135	-
Goblet, 8 oz, 5-3/4" h	30	-	175	-
Iced tea tumbler, 6-1/2" h, ftd	35	-	-	-
Lamp shade, 11-1/2"	100	-	-	-
Nut set	115	-	-	-
Pitcher, 9-1/2" h, ftd	40	-	60	-
Plate, 5-1/2" d, sherbet	20	-	17.50	-
Plate, 7" d	95	-	-	-
Plate, 8" d, luncheon	160	-	115	-
Plate, 9" d, dinner †	70	-	48	-
Salad bowl, 9-1/2" d, ruffled	25	150	20	135
Sandwich plate, 11-3/4" d	48	-	35	-
Sauce, 5" d, ruffled	12.50	-	30	-

Iris, 9" iridescent vase, $45.

Item	Crystal	Green	Iridescent	Pink
Saucer	18	-	12	-
Sherbet, 2-1/2" h, ftd	30	-	20	-
Sherbet, 4" h, ftd	32	-	15.50	-
Soup bowl, 7-1/2" d	195	-	90	-
Sugar, cov	40	150	25	150
Tumbler, 4" h, flat †	150	-	18	-
Tumbler, 6" h, ftd †	25	-	22	-
Tumbler, 6-1/2" h, ftd †	30	-	-	-
Tumbler, flat, water †	165	-	-	-
Vase, 9" h †	32	-	45	225
Wine, 4" h	20	-	33.50	-
Wine, 4-1/4" h, 3 oz	25	-	28	-
Wine, 5-1/2" h	25	-	-	-

Iris, crystal candlesticks $50, and iridescent dinner plate $48.

JUBILEE

Swatches

Pink
Yellow

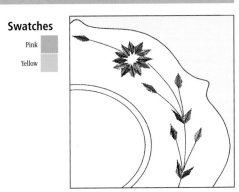

Manufactured by Lancaster Glass Company, Lancaster, Ohio, early 1930s.

Made in pink and yellow.

Item	Pink	Yellow
Bowl, 8" d, 5-1/8" h, three legs	$275	$225
Bowl, 11-1/2" d, three legs	265	250
Bowl, 11-1/2" d, three legs, curved in	-	250
Bowl, 13" d, three legs	250	245
Cake tray, 11" d, two handles	75	85
Candlesticks, pr	190	195
Candy jar, cov, three legs	325	325
Cheese and cracker set	265	255
Cordial, 1 oz, 4" h	-	245
Creamer	45	30
Cup	40	17.50

Item	Pink	Yellow
Fruit bowl, 9" d, handle	-	125
Fruit bowl, 11-1/2" h, flat	200	165
Goblet, 3 oz, 4-7/8" h	-	150
Goblet, 11 oz, 7-1/2" h	-	75
Iced tea tumbler, 12-1/2 oz, 6 1/8" h	-	135
Juice tumbler, 6 oz, 5" h, ftd	-	100
Mayonnaise, plate, orig ladle	315	285
Mayonnaise underplate	125	110

Jubilee, yellow saucer $8, and cup $17.50.

Item	Pink	Yellow
Plate, 7" d, salad	25	16.50
Plate, 8-3/4" d, luncheon	30	16.50
Plate, 14" d, three legs	-	210
Sandwich plate, 13-1/2" d	95	85
Sandwich tray, 11" d, center handle	215	250
Saucer	15	8
Sherbet, 8 oz, 3" h	-	75
Sherbet/champagne, 7 oz, 5-1/2" h	-	75
Sugar	40	24
Tumbler, 10 oz, 6" h, ftd	75	40
Vase, 12" h	-	385

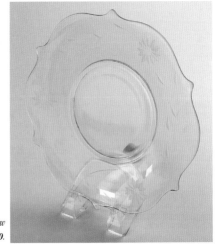

Jubilee, yellow
luncheon plate $16.50.

LACED EDGE

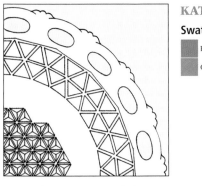

Manufactured by Imperial Glass Company, Bellaire, Ohio, early 1930s.

Made in blue and green with opalescent edges.

Item	Blue	Green
Basket, 9" d	$265	$-
Bowl, 5" d	40	40
Bowl, 5-1/2" d	42	42
Bowl, 5-7/8" d	42	42
Bowl, 11" l, oval	295	285
Bowl, 11" l, oval, divided	165	165
Candlesticks, pr, double lite	175	180
Creamer	45	40
Cup	35	35
Fruit bowl, 4-1/2" d	32	30
Mayonnaise, three pieces	100	125

Item	White
Sugar, ftd	37.50
Vegetable bowl, 9-3/4" l	45

Lake Como, blue and white salad plate $30.

LAUREL

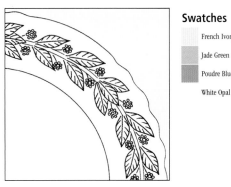

Swatches

French Ivory

Jade Green

Poudre Blue

White Opal

Manufactured by McKee Glass Company, Pittsburgh, Pa., 1930s. Made in French Ivory, Jade Green, Poudre Blue, and White Opal.

Item	French Ivory	Jade Green	Poudre Blue	White Opal
Berry bowl, 4-3/4" d	$9	$15	$16	$14
Berry bowl, 9" d	30	65	60	30
Bowl, 6" d, three legs	15	25	-	15
Bowl, 10-1/2" d, three legs	37.50	50	68	45
Bowl, 11" d	40	55	85	37.50
Candlesticks, pr, 4" h	50	65	-	45
Cereal bowl, 6" d	12	25	28	20
Cheese dish, cov	60	95	-	75
Creamer, short	12	25	-	18
Creamer, tall	15	30	40	24
Cup	9.50	15	20	12

Item	French Ivory	Jade Green	Poudre Blue	White Opal
Plate, 6" d, sherbet	6	15	10	8
Plate, 7-1/2" d, salad	10	20	17.50	12
Plate, 9-1/8" d, dinner	15	25	30	18.50
Plate, 9-1/8" d, grill, round	15	25	-	18.50
Plate, 9-1/8" d, grill, scalloped	15	25	-	18.50
Platter, 10-3/4" l, oval	32	80	45	30
Salt and pepper shakers, pr	60	85	-	65
Saucer	3.25	4.50	7.50	3.50
Sherbet	12.50	20	-	18
Sherbet/champagne, 5"	50	72	-	60
Soup bowl, 7-7/8" d	35	40	-	40
Sugar, short	12	25	-	18
Sugar, tall	15	28	40	24
Tumbler, 9 oz, 4-1/2" h, flat	40	60	-	60
Tumbler, 12 oz, 5" h, flat	60	-	-	-
Vegetable bowl, 9-3/4" l, oval	18.50	480	45	20

Children's

Item	Plain	Green or Decorated	Scotty Dog Green	Scotty Dog Ivory
Creamer	$30	$100	$250	$125
Cup	25	50	100	50
Plate	15	20	75	40
Saucer	12	14	75	40
Sugar	30	100	250	125

Laurel, Jade Green dinner plate $25.

LINCOLN INN

Swatches

Amethyst

Cobalt Blue

Crystal

Red

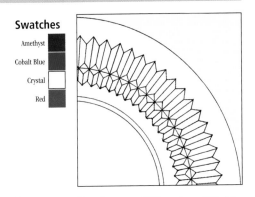

Manufactured by Fenton Art Glass Company, Williamstown, W.V., late 1920s.

Made in amber, amethyst, black, cobalt blue, crystal, green, green opalescent, light blue, opaque jade, pink, and red. Production in black was limited to salt and pepper shakers, valued at $325. Some rare pieces have been identified in several other colors.

Item	Cobalt Blue	Crystal	Other Colors	Red
Ashtray	$17.50	$12	$12	$17.50
Bonbon, oval, handle	17.50	12	14	18
Bonbon, sq, handle	15	12	14	15
Bowl, 6" d, crimped	14.50	7.50	10	14.50
Bowl, 9-1/4" d, ftd	42	18	20	45
Bowl, 10-1/2" d, ftd	50	28	30	50
Candy dish, ftd, oval	24	14.50	14.50	24

Item	Cobalt Blue	Crystal	Other Colors	Red
Cereal bowl, 6" d	12.50	7.50	9.50	12.50
Comport	25	14	15	25
Creamer	24	12	15	24
Cup	17.50	8.50	9.50	18
Finger bowl	20	14	14.50	20
Fruit bowl, 5" d	14	7	9	14
Goblet, 6" h	30	12.50	16	30
Iced tea tumbler, 12 oz, ftd	50	24	28	40
Juice tumbler, 4 oz, flat	35	12	18	30
Nut dish, ftd	20	14.50	16	20
Pitcher, 46 oz, 7-1/4" h	820	700	715	820
Plate, 6" d	19.50	12	12.50	19.50
Plate, 8" d	27.50	15	14	27.50

Lincoln Inn, 8" d pink plate $14.

Item	Cobalt Blue	Crystal	Other Colors	Red
Plate, 9-1/4" d	30	15	16.50	30
Plate, 12" d	35	16	18	35
Salt and pepper shakers, pr	265	175	175	265
Sandwich server, center handle	175	110	110	175
Saucer	5	4	4.50	5
Sherbet, 4-1/2" h, cone shape	18	12	14	18
Sherbet, 4-3/4" h	10	14	20	20
Sugar	18	12	15	24
Tumbler, 5 oz, ftd	24	14	14.50	24
Tumbler, 9 oz, flat	-	14	15	15
Tumbler, 9 oz, ftd	28	32	35	30
Vase, 9-3/4" h	160	85	95	145
Vase, 12" h, ftd	225	115	125	175
Wine	35	20	24	40

Lincoln Inn, cobalt blue goblet $30.

LORAIN

Manufactured by Indiana Glass Company, Dunkirk, Ind., from 1929 to 1939.

Made in crystal, green, and yellow.

Reproductions: † A fantasy sherbet has been reported in both milk white and avocado green.

Item	Crystal	Green	Yellow
Berry bowl, 8" d	**$125**	**$190**	**$250**
Cereal bowl, 6" d	55	65	135
Creamer, ftd	20	20	30
Cup and saucer	32	32	25
Plate, 5-1/2" d, sherbet	10	12	15
Plate, 7-3/4" d, salad	15	18	20
Plate, 8-3/4" d, luncheon	20	24	32.50
Plate, 10-1/4" d, dinner	30	40	90
Platter, 11-1/2" l	32.50	32.50	48

Item	Crystal	Green	Yellow
Relish, 8" d, four parts	20	32	40
Salad bowl, 7-3/4" d	40	40	75
Saucer	6	6	8
Sherbet, ftd †	32	20	40
Snack tray, crystal trim	32	37.50	-
Sugar, ftd	20	24	30
Tumbler, 9 oz, 4-3/4" h, ftd	32	35	40
Vegetable bowl, 9-3/4" l, oval	50	60	65

Lorain, yellow luncheon plate $32.50, and tumbler $40.

Lorain, 6" yellow cereal bowl $135, and green sherbet $20.

MADRID

 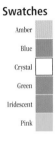

Manufactured by Federal Glass Company, Lancaster, Ohio, from 1932 to 1939.

Made in amber, blue, crystal, green, iridescent, and pink. Iridized pieces are limited to a console set, consisting of a low bowl and pair of candlesticks, valued at $40.

Reproductions: † Reproductions include candlesticks, cups, saucers and vegetable bowl. Reproductions are found in amber, blue, crystal, and pink. Federal Glass Company reissued this pattern under the name "Recollection." Some of these pieces were dated 1976. When Federal went bankrupt, the molds were sold to Indiana Glass, which removed the date and began production of crystal, then pink. Several pieces were made recently that were not part of the original production and include a footed cake stand, goblet, two-section grill plate, preserves stand, squatty salt and pepper shakers, 11-oz tumbler and vase.

Item	Amber	Blue	Crystal	Green	Pink
Ashtray, 6" sq	$300	$-	$-	$295	$-
Berry bowl, small	10	-	6.50	-	-
Berry bowl, 9-3/8" d	25	-	25	-	25
Bowl, 7" d	17.50	-	12	17.50	-
Butter dish, cov	85	-	65	90	-
Cake plate, 11-1/4" d	24	-	20	-	20
Candlesticks, 2-1/4" h, pr †	18.50	-	14.50	-	28
Coaster, 5" d	40	-	40	35	-
Console bowl, 11" d	15	-	18	-	36
Cookie jar	50	-	45	-	40
Creamer	30	18	7	20	-
Cream soup, 4 3/4" d	25	-	15.50	-	-
Cup †	10	20	6.50	12	8.50
Gravy boat	1,950	-	900	-	-
Gravy boat platter	900	-	900	-	-
Hot dish coaster, 3-1/2" d	195	-	40	45	-
Iced tea tumbler, round	25	-	24	22	-
Jam dish, 7" d	24	35	12	25	-
Juice pitcher	50	-	45	-	-
Juice tumbler, 5 oz, 3-7/8" h, ftd	18	45	40	35	-
Pitcher, jug-type	60	-	24	190	-
Pitcher, 60 oz, 8" h, sq	55	225	150	145	50
Pitcher, 80 oz, 8-1/2" h, ice lip	75	-	30	225	-
Plate, 6" d, sherbet	5.50	12	4	4.50	4
Plate, 7-1/2" d, salad	15	17	12	9	9
Plate, 8-7/8" d, luncheon	10	20	7.50	12	10
Plate, 10-1/2" d, dinner	48	60	24	45	-

Item	Amber	Blue	Crystal	Green	Pink
Plate, 10-1/2" d, grill	12	-	10	18.50	-
Platter, 11-1/2" oval	20	32	20	18	18
Relish dish, 10-1/2" d	14.50	-	7	16	20
Salad bowl, 8" d	17	-	9.50	15.50	-
Salad bowl, 9-1/2" d	32	-	30	-	-
Salt and pepper shakers, 3-1/2" h	135	145	95	110	-
Sauce bowl, 5" d	12	-	7.50	8.50	11
Saucer †	5	8	4	7	5
Sherbet, cone	5.50	18	6.50	14	-
Sherbet, ftd	10	15	6	12	-
Soup bowl, 7" d †	20	20	6	15.50	-
Sugar, cov †	65	175	32.50	80	-

Madrid, amber sugar $20, and creamer $30.

Item	Amber	Blue	Crystal	Green	Pink
Sugar, open †	20	15	8	20	-
Tumbler, 9 oz, 4-1/2" h	18	40	17.50	25	22.50
Tumbler, 12 oz, 5-1/4" h, ftd or flat	30	-	30	45	-
Vegetable bowl, 10" l, oval †	30	35	25	25	30

Madrid, amber grill plate $12, berry bowl $10, and cup $10.

Madrid, amber bowl $17.50.

MANHATTAN

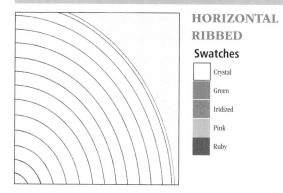

HORIZONTAL RIBBED

Swatches

- ☐ Crystal
- ☐ Green
- ☐ Iridized
- ☐ Pink
- ☐ Ruby

Manufactured by Anchor Hocking Glass Company, from 1938 to 1943.

Made in crystal, green, iridized, pink, and ruby. Ruby pieces are limited to relish tray inserts, currently valued at $10 each. Green and iridized production was limited to footed tumblers, currently valued at $17.50.

Anchor Hocking introduced a similar pattern, Park Avenue, in 1987. Anchor Hocking was careful to preserve the Manhattan pattern. Collectors should pay careful attention to measurements if they are uncertain of the pattern.

Item	Crystal	Pink
Ashtray, 4" d, round	$15	$10
Ashtray, 4-1/2" w, sq	20	-
Berry bowl, 5-3/8" d, handles	24	25

Item	Crystal	Pink
Berry bowl, 7-1/2" d	28	-
Bowl, 4-1/2" d	12.50	-
Bowl, 8" d, closed handles	28	25
Bowl, 8" d, metal handle	35	-
Bowl, 9-1/2" d, handle	-	45
Candlesticks, pr, 4-1/2" h	20	-
Candy dish, three legs	-	18
Candy dish, cov	40	-
Cereal bowl, 5-1/4" d, no handles	120	-
Coaster, 3-1/2"	30	-
Cocktail	18	-
Comport, 5-3/4" h	35	60
Creamer, oval	9	20
Cup	22	160
Fruit bowl, 9-1/2" d, two open handles	40	50
Juice pitcher, 24 oz	55	-
Pitcher, 80 oz, tilted	55	85
Plate, 6" d, sherbet	12	50
Plate, 8-1/2" d, salad	20	-
Plate, 10-1/4" d, dinner	25	120
Relish tray insert	2.50	10
Relish tray, 14" d, inserts	110	50
Relish tray, 14" d, four parts	95	-
Salad bowl, 9" d	20	-
Salt and pepper shakers, pr, 2" h, sq	50	60
Sandwich plate, 14" d	22	-
Sauce bowl, 4-1/2" d, handles	10	-
Saucer	7	50
Sherbet	12.50	20

Item	Crystal	Pink
Sugar, oval	15	17.50
Tumbler, 10 oz, 5-1/4" h, ftd	22	27.50
Vase, 8" h	30	-
Wine, 3-1/2" h	8	-

Manhattan, relish tray with ruby inserts and crystal base $95,
crystal comport $35, vase $30, and fruit bowl with open handles $40.

Manhattan, small crystal bowl (on pedestal) $12.50; pink creamer $20 and sugar $17.50; crystal salt and pepper shakers $50; crystal cereal bowl $120; crystal tumbler $22; crystal pitcher $55; bowl with metal stand $35; and pink ftd candy dish $18.

MAYFAIR, FEDERAL

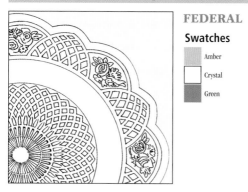

FEDERAL

Swatches

▨	Amber
☐	Crystal
▨	Green

Manufactured by Federal Glass Company, Columbus, Ohio, 1934. Made in amber, crystal, and green.

Item	Amber	Crystal	Green
Cereal bowl, 6" d	$18.50	$15	$22
Cream soup, 5" d	22	12	20
Creamer, ftd	17.50	14	16
Cup	8.50	5	8.50
Plate, 6-3/4" d, salad	7	4.50	8.50
Plate, 9-1/2" d, dinner	16.50	12	14.50
Plate, 9-1/2" d, grill	17.50	15	17.50
Platter, 12" l, oval	27.50	22	30
Sauce bowl, 5" d	8.50	7	12
Saucer	4.50	2.50	4.50
Sugar, ftd	12	10	12

Item	Amber	Crystal	Green
Tumbler, 9 oz, 4-1/2" h	27.50	16.50	32
Vegetable, 10" l, oval	32	32	32

Mayfair, amber dinner plate $16.50.

MAYFAIR, HOCKING

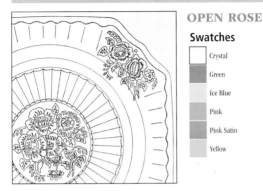

Swatches

	Crystal
	Green
	Ice Blue
	Pink
	Pink Satin
	Yellow

Manufactured by Hocking Glass Company, Lancaster, Ohio, from 1931 to 1937.

Made in crystal, green, ice blue, pink, pink satin, and yellow.

Reproductions: † This pattern has been plagued with reproductions since 1977. Items reproduced include cookie jars, salt and pepper shakers, juice pitchers, and whiskey glasses. Reproductions are found in amethyst, blue, cobalt blue, green, pink, and red.

Item	Crystal	Green	Ice Blue	Pink	Pink Satin	Yellow
Bowl, 11-3/4" l, flat	$-	$35	$75	$85	$70	$195
Butter dish, cov	-	1,295	350	80	95	1,295
Cake plate, 10" d, ftd	-	115	90	40	45	-

Item	Crystal	Green	Ice Blue	Pink	Pink Satin	Yellow
Cake plate, 12" d, handles	-	40	95	50	50	-
Candy dish, cov	-	575	325	70	85	475
Celery dish, 9" l, divided	-	155	75	-	-	150
Celery dish, 10" l, divided	-	-	90	295	-	-
Celery dish, 10" l, not divided	-	115	80	65	50	115
Cereal bowl, 5-1/2" d	-	24	48	35	35	75
Claret, 4-1/2 oz, 5-1/4" h	-	950	-	1,150	-	-
Cocktail, 3 oz, 4" h	-	975	-	130	-	-

Mayfair, pink 11 oz tumbler $225, and pink satin-finish covered cookie jar $40.

Item	Crystal	Green	Ice Blue	Pink	Pink Satin	Yellow
Console bowl, 9" d, 3-1/8" h, three legs	-	5,000	-	5,000	-	-
Cookie jar, cov †	-	575	295	75	40	860
Cordial, 1 oz, 3-3/4" h	-	950		1,100	-	-
Cream soup, 5" d	-	-	-	65	68	-
Creamer, ftd	-			40	30	
Cup	-	150	55	20	27.50	150
Decanter, stopper, 32 oz	-	-		275	-	-
Fruit bowl, 12" d, scalloped	-	50	125	95	75	215
Goblet, 2-1/2 oz, 4-1/8"	-	950		950	-	-
Goblet, 9 oz, 5-3/4" h	-	465	-	80	-	-
Goblet, 9 oz, 7-1/4" h, thin	-	-	225	475	-	-
Iced tea tumbler, 13-1/2 oz, 5-1/4" h			225	80		
Iced tea tumbler, 15 oz, 6-1/2" h, ftd	-	250	285	45	65	-

Item	Crystal	Green	Ice Blue	Pink	Pink Satin	Yellow
Juice pitcher, 37 oz, 6" h †	24.50	525	150	85	65	525
Juice tumbler, 3 oz, 3-1/4" h, ftd	-	-	-	80	-	-
Juice tumbler, 5 oz, 3-1/2" h	-	-	225	80	-	-
Pitcher, 60 oz, 8" h	-	475	195	85	100	425
Pitcher, 80 oz, 8-1/2" h	-	725	225	135	135	725
Plate, 5-3/4" d	-	90	25	20	15	90
Plate, 6-1/2" d, off-center indent	-	115	44	30	35	-

Mayfair, ice blue handled vegetable bowl $75.

Item	Crystal	Green	Ice Blue	Pink	Pink Satin	Yellow
Plate, 6-1/2" d, sherbet	-	-	24	20	-	-
Plate, 8-1/2" d, luncheon	-	85	70	35	35	80
Plate, 9-1/2" d, dinner	-	150	100	70	65	150
Plate, 9-1/2" d, grill	-	75	70	50	35	80
Plate, 11-1/2" d, grill, handles	-	-	-	-	-	100
Platter, 12" l, oval, open handles	17.50	175	60	35	35	115

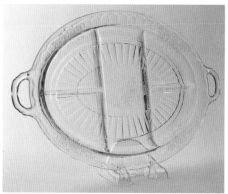

Mayfair, crystal, platter, oval, open handles $17.50.

Item	Crystal	Green	Ice Blue	Pink	Pink Satin	Yellow
Platter, 12-1/2" oval, 8" wide, closed handles	-	245	-	-	-	245
Relish, 8-3/8" d, four parts	-	160	65	37.50	37.50	160
Relish, 8-3/8" d, non-partitioned	-	275	-	200	-	275
Salt and pepper shakers, pr, flat †	20	1,000	175	65	70	800
Sandwich server, center handle	-	40	85	50	50	130

REPRODUCTION! Mayfair, green and blue cookie jars.

Item	Crystal	Green	Ice Blue	Pink	Pink Satin	Yellow
Saucer	-	90	30	45	35	140
Sherbet, 2-1/4" flat	-	-	135	185	-	-
Sherbet, 3" ftd	-	-	-	20	-	-
Sherbet, 4-3/4" ftd	-	150	75	185	75	150
Sugar, ftd	-	195	85	38	40	185
Sweet pea vase	-	285	150	250	145	-
Tumbler, 9 oz, 4-1/4" h	-	-	100	30	-	-
Tumbler, 10 oz, 5-1/4" h	-	-	145	65	-	185
Tumbler, 11 oz, 4-3/4" h	-	200	250	225	225	215
Vegetable bowl, 7" d, two handles	-	33	75	60	70	195
Vegetable bowl, 9-1/2" l, oval	-	110	75	45	30	125
Vegetable bowl, 10" d cov	-	-	120	150	120	900
Vegetable bowl, 10" d open	-	-	85	48.50	20	200
Whiskey, 1-1/2 oz, 2-1/4" h †	-	-	-	58	-	-
Wine, 3 oz, 4-1/2" h	-	450	-	120	-	-

MELBA

Swatches

Amethyst

Black

Green

Pink

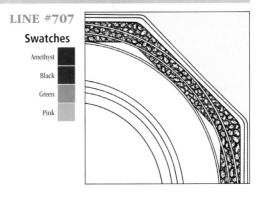

Manufactured by L.E. Smith Glass Company, Mount Pleasant, Pa., in the early 1930s.

Made in amethyst, black, green, and pink.

Item	Amethyst	Black	Green	Pink
Baker, oval	$20	$22	$18	$18
Bowl, 10-1/2" d, ruffled	18	20	15	15
Candleholder	15	17	12	12
Creamer	15	18	12	12
Cup	6.50	8.50	5	5
Dessert bowl	4.50	5	3.50	3.50
Plate, 6" d, bread and butter	5	7.50	4	4
Plate, 7" d, salad	7	9.50	6	6
Plate, 9" d, luncheon	9	12	8	8
Platter	15	18	12	12
Salad bowl	18	20	15	15

Item	Amethyst	Black	Green	Pink
Saucer	3.50	4.50	3	3
Serving plate, 9" d, handles	15	18	12	12
Sugar	15	18	12	12
Vegetable bowl, 9-1/2" l	18	20	15	15

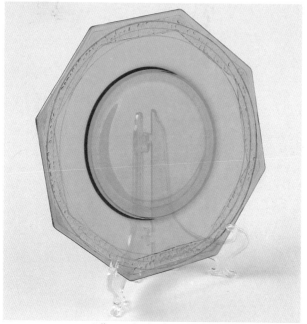

Melba, amethyst luncheon plate $9.

DIAMOND PATTERN

Swatches

Crystal

Green

Ice Blue

Jade-ite

Pink

Royal Ruby

Manufactured by Hocking Glass Company, Lancaster, Ohio, from 1935 to 1938.

Made in crystal, green, ice blue, jade-ite, pink, and royal ruby.

Reproductions: † Reproductions include the butter dish, creamer, 8" pitcher, salt and pepper shakers, sugar, and tumbler. Reproductions are found in amberina, blue, cobalt blue, crystal, green, pink, and red.

Item	Crystal	Green	Ice Blue	Pink	Royal Ruby
Berry bowl, 4-1/2" d	$-	$25	$-	$-	$-
Bowl, 8" d, curved at top	48	-	-	95	-
Bowl, 8" d, straight sides	-	-	-	110	-
Bowl, 11" d, shallow	-	-	-	-	850
Butter dish, cov †	300	-	-	575	-

Item	Crystal	Green	Ice Blue	Pink	Royal Ruby
Cake plate, 12" d, ftd	40	-	-	45	-
Candy jar, cov, 11-1/2"	125	-	-	200	-
Celery dish, 10-1/2" l, oval	19.50	-	160	45	-
Cereal bowl, 6-1/4" d	15	18	-	35	-
Coaster, 5-3/4" d	19.50	-	-	45	-
Comport, 5" d	18	-	-	50	-
Creamer, ftd †	12.50	-	-	24	215
Cup	11	20	14	30	235
Fruit bowl, 8-3/4" d	40	-	-	60	450
Goblet, 10 oz, 5-1/2" h	30	-	-	75	250
Iced tea tumbler, 14 oz, 5-3/4" h	25	-	-	85	-
Juice goblet, 5 oz, 4-3/4" h	35	-	-	115	250
Juice tumbler, 5 oz, 4" h	27.50	-	150	60	200
Pitcher, 65 oz, 8-1/2" h, ice lip	75	-	-	295	50
Plate, 5-3/4" d, sherbet	10	9	55	16	-
Plate, 8-1/2" d, salad	15	14	-	60	150
Plate, 10-1/4" d, dinner	25	-	150	45	-
Plate, 10-1/4" d, grill	12	-	-	50	-
Platter, 12-1/4" l, oval	18	-	-	95	-
Relish, 8-3/4" l, 4 part	30	-	-	30	-
Relish, 11-3/4" d, divided	50	-	-	40	-
Salt and pepper shakers, pr †	40	300	-	95	-
Saucer	4	-	-	10	60
Sherbet	10	-	60	20	175
Sugar †	12	-	-	25	225
Tumbler, 10 oz, 4-1/2" h, flat †	20	45	-	40	-

Item	Crystal	Green	Ice Blue	Pink	Royal Ruby
Tumbler, 14 oz, 5-3/4" h	28	-	-	-	-
Vegetable bowl, 10" l, oval	20	-	-	70	-
Whiskey	24	-	-	-	-
Wine, 3 oz, 3-3/4" h	25	-	-	85	250

*Miss America, pink goblet $75, comport $50,
and tumbler 10 oz, with original label $45.*

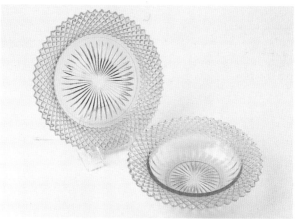

Miss America, green plate $9, and berry bowl $25.

Miss America, 10" pink oval vegetable bowl $70.

MOONDROPS

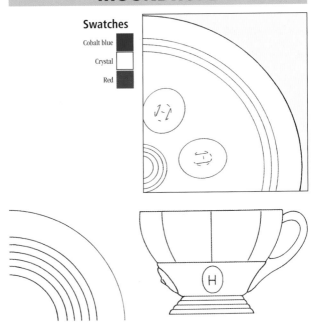

Swatches

Cobalt blue

Crystal

Red

Manufactured by New Martinsville Glass Company, New Martinsville, W.V., from 1932 to 1940.

Made in amber, amethyst, black, cobalt blue, crystal, dark green, green, ice blue, Jade-ite, light green, pink, red, and smoke.

Item	Cobalt Blue	Crystal	Other Colors	Red
Ashtray	$30	$-	$18	$35
Berry bowl, 5-1/4" d	20	-	12	20
Bowl, 8-1/2" d, ftd, concave top	40	-	25	40
Bowl, 9-1/2" d, three legs, ruffled	60	-	-	60
Bowl, 9-3/4" l, oval, handles	50	-	30	50
Butter dish, cov	425	-	275	295
Candlesticks, pr, 2" h, ruffled	40	-	25	40
Candlesticks, pr, 4" h, sherbet style	30	-	18	30
Candlesticks, pr, 5" h, ruffled	32	-	22	32
Candlesticks, pr, 5" h, wings	90	-	60	90
Candlesticks, pr, 5-1/4" h, triple light	100	65	65	100
Candlesticks, pr, 8-1/2" h, metal stem	40	-	32	40
Candy dish, 8" d, ruffled	40	-	20	40
Casserole, cov, 9-3/4" d	185	-	100	185
Celery bowl, 11" l, boat-shape	30	-	24	30
Cocktail shaker, metal top	60	-	35	60
Comport, 4" d	25	-	15	25
Comport, 11-1/2" d	60	-	30	60
Console bowl, 13" d, wings	-	-	80	120
Cordial, 3/4 oz, 2-7/8" h	55	-	25	48
Cream soup, 4-1/4" d	90	-	35	90
Creamer, 2-3/4" h	15	-	10	25
Creamer, 3-3/4" h	12	-	12	16
Cup	16	8	10	16
Decanter, 7-3/4" h	70	-	40	70
Decanter, 10-1/4" h, rocket-shape	425	-	375	425
Goblet, 5 oz, 4-3/4" h	25	-	15	22

Item	Cobalt Blue	Crystal	Other Colors	Red
Goblet, 8 oz, 5-3/4" h	35	-	20	33
Goblet, 9 oz, 6-1/4" h, metal stem	15	-	17.50	15
Gravy boat	120	-	90	125
Juice tumbler, 3 oz, 3-1/4" h, ftd	15	-	10	15
Mayonnaise, 5-1/4" h	32.50	-	30	32.50
Mug, 12 oz, 5-1/8" h	40	-	24	42
Perfume bottle, rocket-shape	200	-	150	210

Moondrops, pink saucer $4, and cup $10.

Item	Cobalt Blue	Crystal	Other Colors	Red
Pickle, 7-1/2" d	25	-	15	25
Pitcher, 22 oz, 6-7/8" h	175	-	90	175
Pitcher, 32 oz, 8-1/8" h	195	-	110	195
Pitcher, 50 oz, 8" h, lip	200	-	115	200
Pitcher, 53 oz, 8-1/8" h	195	-	120	195
Plate, 5-7/8" d	12	-	7.50	12
Plate, 6" d, round, off center indent	12.50	-	10	12.50
Plate, 6-1/8" d, sherbet	8	-	6	8
Plate, 7-1/8" d, salad	12	-	10	12
Plate, 8-1/2" d, luncheon	20	-	12	15
Plate, 9-1/2" d, dinner	25	-	15	25
Platter, 12" l, oval	35	-	20	35
Powder jar, three ftd	175	-	100	185
Relish, 8-1/2" d, 3 ftd, divided	30	-	20	30
Sandwich plate, 14" d	40	-	20	40
Sandwich plate, 14" d, with handles	44	-	24	45
Saucer	6	2	4	8.50
Sherbet, 2-5/8" h	15	10	11	20
Sherbet, 3-1/2" h	35	-	15	25
Shot glass, 2 oz, 2-3/4" h	17.50	-	12	24.50
Shot glass, 2 oz, 2-3/4" h, handle	17.50	-	12	17.50
Soup bowl, 6-3/4" d	80	-	-	80
Sugar, 2-3/4" h	12	-	12	20
Tray, 7-1/2" l	15	-	20	16
Tumbler, 5 oz, 3-5/8" h	15	-	10	15
Tumbler, 8 oz, 4-3/8" h	17.50	-	12	22
Tumbler, 9 oz, 4-7/8" h, handle	30	-	15	28
Tumbler, 12 oz, 5-1/8" h	30	-	15	35
Vase, 7-1/4" h, flat, ruffled	60	-	60	60

Item	Cobalt Blue	Crystal	Other Colors	Red
Vase, 8-1/2" h, bud, rocket-shape	245	-	185	245
Vase, 9-1/4" h, rocket-shape	240	-	125	240
Vegetable bowl, 9-3/4" l, oval	48	-	24	48
Wine, 4-3/4" h, rocket-shape	27.50	-	30	85
Wine, 4 oz, 5-1/2" h, metal stem	20	-	12	20

Moondrops, ruby sugar $20, and creamer $16.

MOONSTONE

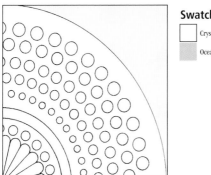

Swatches

☐ Crystal

▨ Ocean Green

Manufactured by Anchor Hocking Glass Company, Lancaster, Ohio, from 1941 to 1946.

Made in crystal with opalescent hobnails and Ocean Green with opalescent hobnails.

Item	Crystal	Ocean Green
Berry bowl, 5-1/2" d	$25	$-
Bonbon, heart shape, handle	15	-
Bowl, 6-1/2" d, crimped, handle	20	-
Bowl, 7-1/4" d, flat	25	-
Bowl, 9-1/2" d, crimped	25	-
Bud vase, 5-1/2" h	18	-
Candleholder, pr	20	-
Candy jar, cov, 6" h	30	-
Cigarette box, cov	25	-

Item	Crystal	Ocean Green
Creamer	10	9.50
Cup	8	10
Dessert bowl, 5-1/2" d, crimped	12.50	-
Goblet, 10 oz	20	24
Plate, 6-1/4" d, sherbet	7	9
Plate, 8-3/8" d, luncheon	17.50	17.50
Puff box, cov, 4-3/4" d, round	25	-
Relish, 7-1/4" d, divided	12	-
Relish, cloverleaf	14	-
Sandwich plate, 10-3/4" d	45	-
Saucer	6	6
Sherbet, ftd	7.50	7
Sugar, ftd	10	12.50
Vase, 6-1/2" h, ruffled	24	-

Moonstone, crystal luncheon plate with opalescent hobnails $17.50.

MOROCCAN AMETHYST

Swatches

Amethyst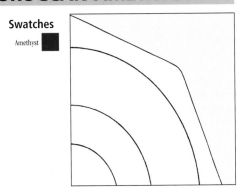

Manufactured by Hazel Ware, division of Continental Can, 1960s.
Made in amethyst.

Item	Amethyst
Ashtray, 3-1/4" d, round	$5.75
Ashtray, 3-1/4" w, triangular	5.75
Ashtray, 6-7/8" w, triangular	12.50
Ashtray, 8" w, square	14
Bowl, 5-3/4" w, deep, square	12
Bowl, 6" d, round	12.50
Bowl, 7-3/4" l, oval	168
Bowl, 7-3/4" l, rectangular, metal handle	17.50
Bowl, 10-3/4" d	30
Candy, cov, short	35
Candy, cov, tall	32
Chip and dip, 10-3/4" and 5-3/4" bowls in metal frame	40

Item	Amethyst
Cocktail shaker, chrome lid	30
Cocktail, stirrer, 16 oz, 6-1/4" h, lip	30
Cup	7.50
Fruit bowl, 4-3/4" d, octagonal	9
Goblet, 9 oz, 5-1/2" h	12.50
Ice bucket, 6" h	50
Iced tea tumbler, 16 oz, 6-1/2" h	18.50
Juice goblet, 5-1/2 oz, 4-3/8" h	12
Juice tumbler, 4 oz, 2-1/2" h	12
Old fashioned tumbler, 8 oz, 3-1/4" h	12.50
Plate, 5-3/4" d, sherbet	4.50
Plate, 7-1/4" d, salad	7
Plate, 9-3/4" d, dinner	9
Punch bowl	85
Punch cup	6
Relish, 7-3/4" l	14
Salad fork and spoon	12
Sandwich plate, 12" d, metal handle	15
Saucer	3
Sherbet, 7-1/2 oz, 4-1/4" h	7.50
Snack plate, 10" l, fan shaped, cup rest	8
Snack set, square plate, cup	12
Tidbit, three tiers	75
Tumbler, 9 oz	10
Tumbler, 11 oz, 4-1/4" h, crinkled bottom	12
Tumbler, 11 oz, 4-5/8" h	12
Vase, 8-1/2" h, ruffled	40
Wine, 4-1/2 oz, 4" h	10

Moroccan Amethyst, cup $7.50, and saucer $3.

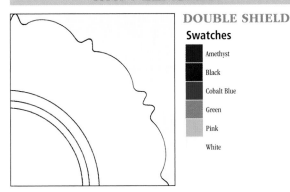

DOUBLE SHIELD

Swatches

	Amethyst
	Black
	Cobalt Blue
	Green
	Pink
	White

Manufactured by L.E. Smith, Mt. Pleasant, Pa., from the 1920s to 1934.

Made in amethyst, black, cobalt blue, crystal, green, pink, and white.

Item	Ameth.	Black	Cobalt Blue	Green	Pink
Bonbon, 7" d, rolled edge	$24	$24.50	$24	$16	$16
Bowl, 6" d, three legs	-	25	-	-	-
Bowl, 6" w, sq, handles	27.50	18	24	15	15
Bowl, 7" d, three ftd, rolled out edge	18.50	24.50	18.50	17.50	17.50
Bowl, 8" d, scalloped, two handles	37.50	35	37.50	20	20
Bowl, 8" d, sq, two handles	38	40	38	20	20
Bowl, 9" d, scalloped, 1-3/4" deep, ftd	28	32	30	-	-

Item	Ameth.	Black	Cobalt Blue	Green	Pink
Cake plate, 10-1/2" d, 1-1/4" h, ftd	45	47	40	-	-
Cake plate, 10-1/2" d, two handles	26	40	28	17.50	17.50
Candlesticks, pr, single lite	28	42.50	30	24	28
Candlesticks, pr, two lite	50	50	60	30	32
Creamer	21	20	22.50	20	24
Cup	15	15	14	12.50	12.50
Fruit bowl, 4-7/8" sq	16	20	18	12	12.50
Fruit bowl, 9-1/4" sq	30	50	35	20	20
Fruit bowl, 10" d, scalloped	40	40	40	-	-
Leaf, 8" l	12.50	17.50	16	-	-
Leaf, 11-1/4" l	25	30	28	-	-
Mayonnaise, 5-1/2" h, three ftd	25	30	35	17.50	17.50
Mint, 6" d, center handle	25	27.50	30	16	16
Plate, 8" d, scalloped	16	15	16	12.50	12.50
Plate, 8" d, scalloped, three ftd	17.50	27	17.50	12.50	12.50
Plate, 8" w, sq	17.50	25	17.50	12.50	12.50
Plate, 12" d, two handles	35	35	35	20	20
Salt and pepper shakers, pr	50	50	45	25	25
Sandwich server, center handle	40	37.50	40	-	-
Saucer	5	5	5	3.50	3.50
Sherbet	15	15	18	12.50	12.50
Sugar	9	22.50	22	20	20
Tumbler, ftd	25	27.50	32.50	-	-
Vase, 7-1/4" h	30	35	40	-	35

Mt. Pleasant, black creamer $20, sugar (on pedestal) $22.50, cup $15, and bowl with handles $40.

NATIONAL

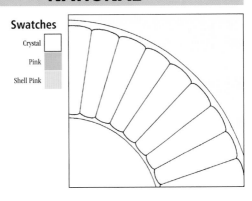

Swatches

Crystal

Pink

Shell Pink

Manufactured by Jeannette Glass Company, Jeannette, Pa., from the late 1940s to the mid-1950s.

Made in crystal, pink, and shell pink. Collector interest is primarily with crystal. Prices for pink and shell pink are not yet firmly established, but usually command slightly higher than crystal.

Item	Crystal
Ashtray	$4.50
Berry bowl, 4-1/2" d	4
Berry bowl, 8-1/2" d	8
Bowl, 12" d	15
Candleholders, pr	30
Candy dish, cov, ftd	20
Cigarette box	15
Creamer	5

Item	Crystal
Creamer and sugar tray	6
Cup	4
Jar, cov	15
Lazy Susan	40
Milk pitcher, 20 oz	20
Plate, 8" d	6.50
Punch bowl stand	10
Punch bowl, 12" d	25
Punch cup	3.50
Relish, three parts	15
Salt and pepper shakers, pr	10
Saucer	1

National, crystal candleholders $30.

Item	Crystal
Sugar, open	6.50
Serving plate, 15" d	17.50
Tray, two handles	17.50
Tumbler, ftd	8.50
Vase, 9"	20
Water pitcher, 64 oz	30

National, crystal sugar bowl $6.50.

NEW CENTURY

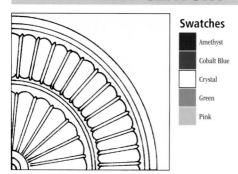

Swatches

- ■ Amethyst
- ■ Cobalt Blue
- □ Crystal
- ■ Green
- ■ Pink

Manufactured by Hazel Atlas Company, Clarksburg, W.V., and Zanesville, Ohio, from 1930 to 1935.

Made in crystal and green, with limited production in amethyst, cobalt blue, and pink.

Item	Ameth.	Cobalt Blue	Crystal	Green	Pink
Ashtray/coaster, 5-3/8" d	$-	$-	$30	$30	$-
Berry bowl, 4-1/2" d	-	-	35	35	-
Berry bowl, 8" d	-	-	30	30	-
Butter dish, cov	-	-	75	75	-
Casserole, cov, 9" d	-	-	115	115	-
Cocktail, 3-1/4 oz	-	-	42	42	-
Cream soup, 4-3/4" d	-	-	25	25	-
Creamer	-	-	12	14	-
Cup	20	20	10	12	20

Item	Ameth.	Cobalt Blue	Crystal	Green	Pink
Decanter, stopper	-	-	90	90	-
Pitcher, with or without ice lip, 60 oz	55	55	45	48	50
Pitcher, with or without ice lip, 80 oz	55	55	45	48	50
Plate, 6" d, sherbet	-	-	6	6.50	-
Plate, 8-1/2" d, salad	-	-	10	12	-
Plate, 10" d, dinner	-	-	24	24	-
Plate, 10" d, grill	-	-	15	18	-
Platter, 11" l, oval	-	-	30	30	-
Salt and pepper shakers, pr	-	-	45	45	-

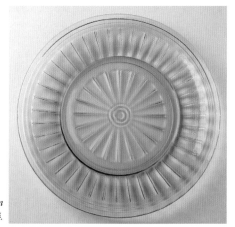

New Century, green dinner plate $24.

Item	Ameth.	Cobalt Blue	Crystal	Green	Pink
Saucer	7.50	7.50	5	6.50	8
Sherbet, 3" h	-	-	9	9	-
Sugar, cov	-	-	40	45	-
Tumbler, 5 oz, 3-1/2" h	12	16.50	15	18	18
Tumbler, 5 oz, 4" h, ftd	-	-	30	32.50	-
Tumbler, 8 oz, 3-1/2" h	-	-	25	27.50	-
Tumbler, 9 oz, 4-1/4" h	15	20	24	18	15
Tumbler, 9 oz, 4-7/8" h, ftd	-	-	25	25	-
Whiskey, 2-1/2" h, 1-1/2 oz	-	-	18	20	-
Wine, 2-1/2 oz	-	-	35	40	-

New Century, green salt and pepper shakers $45.

NEWPORT

HAIRPIN

Swatches

Amethyst

Cobalt Blue

Pink

Platonite White

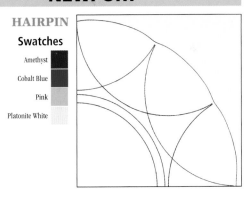

Manufactured by Hazel Atlas Glass Company, Clarksburg, W.V., and Zanesville, Ohio, from 1936 to the early 1950s.

Made in amethyst, cobalt blue, pink (from 1936 to 1940), Platonite white, and fired-on colors (from the 1940s to early 1950s).

Item	Ameth.	Cobalt Blue	Fired-On	Pink	Platon.
Berry bowl, 8-1/4" d	$50	$50	$16	$25	$10
Cream soup, 4-3/4" d	25	25	10	17.50	8.50
Creamer	20	20	8.50	10	6
Cup	12	15	9.50	9	6.50
Plate, 6" d, sherbet	7.50	10	5	3.50	2
Plate, 8-1/2" d, luncheon	15	22	8	8	6.50
Plate, 8-13/16" d, dinner	32	35	15	15	12
Platter, 11-3/4" l, oval	42	55	18	20	12

Newport, cobalt blue cup $15, and 4-1/2" cobalt blue flat tumbler $50.

Item	Ameth.	Cobalt Blue	Fired-On	Pink	Platon.
Salt and pepper shakers, pr	60	65	32	30	15
Saucer	5.25	6	3	2.50	2
Sherbet	15	16.50	10	8	4
Sugar	20	20	9.50	10	8
Tumbler, 9 oz, 4-1/2" h	42	50	18.50	20	-

Newport, amethyst dinner plate $32, sugar $20, creamer $20, and cream soup bowl $25.

NORMANDIE

BOUQUET AND LATTICE

Swatches

	Amber
	Crystal
	Iridescent
	Pink

Manufactured by Federal Glass Company, Columbus, Ohio, from 1933 to 1940.

Made in amber, crystal, iridescent, and pink.

Item	Amber	Crystal	Iridescent	Pink
Berry bowl, 5" d	$9.50	$6	$7.50	$14
Berry bowl, 8-1/2" d	35	24	30	80
Cereal bowl, 6-1/2" d	30	20	12	35
Creamer, ftd	20	10	10	15
Cup	7.50	4	10	12.50
Iced tea tumbler, 12 oz, 5" h	45	-	-	-
Juice tumbler, 5 oz, 4" h	40	-	-	-
Pitcher, 80 oz, 8" h	115	-	-	245
Plate, 7-3/4" d, salad	13	5	55	14
Plate, 9-1/4" d, luncheon	25	6	16.50	100
Plate, 11" d, dinner	55	15	12	18

Item	Amber	Crystal	Iridescent	Pink
Plate, 11" d, grill	15	8	8	25
Platter, 11-3/4" l	24	10	12	80
Salt and pepper shakers, pr	50	20	-	4
Saucer	4	1.50	2.50	10
Sherbet	7.50	6	7.50	9.50
Sugar	10	6	9.50	12
Tumbler, 9 oz, 4-1/4" h	25	10	-	50
Vegetable bowl, 10" l, oval	27.50	12	25	45

*Normandie,
iridescent dinner
plate $12.*

OLD CAFÉ

Swatches

Crystal

Pink

Royal Ruby

Manufactured by Hocking Glass Company, Lancaster, Ohio, from 1936 to 1940.

Made in crystal, pink, and royal ruby.

Item	Crystal	Pink	Royal Ruby
Berry bowl, 3-3/4" d	$9.50	$10	$9
Bowl, 6-1/2" d	15	18	-
Bowl, 9" d, closed handles	12	10	15
Candy dish, 8" d, low	12.50	18.50	20

Old Café, 5" two-handled covered dish with pink base and royal ruby lid $30.

Old Café, ruby bowl with handles and original label **$15**.

Item	Crystal	Pink	Royal Ruby
Candy jar, 5-1/2" d, crystal with ruby cover	-	-	30
Cereal bowl, 5-1/2" d	30	30	30
Cup	12	16	12
Juice tumbler, 3" h	18	25	20
Lamp	100	100	150
Olive dish, 6" l, oblong	7.50	10	-
Pitcher, 36 oz, 6" h	125	145	-
Plate, 6" d, sherbet	5	5	-
Plate, 10" d, dinner	60	65	-
Saucer	5	5	-
Sherbet, low, ftd	7.50	18	12
Tumbler, 4" h	18	20	18
Vase, 7-1/4" h	25	45	50

Old Café, ruby berry bowl $9.

OLD COLONY

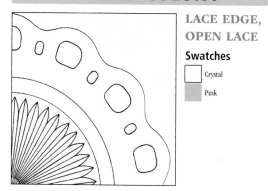

**LACE EDGE,
OPEN LACE**

Swatches

	Crystal
	Pink

Manufactured by Hocking Glass Company, Lancaster, Ohio, from 1935 to 1938.

Made in crystal and pink.

Crystal Old Colony pieces are valued at about 50 percent of pink, as are frosted or satin finish prices. Many other companies made a look-alike to Old Colony, so care must be exercised.

Item	Pink
Bonbon, cov	$65
Bowl, 9-1/2" d, plain	32.50
Bowl, 9-1/2" d, ribbed	35
Butter dish, cov	100
Candlesticks, pr	350
Candy jar, cov, ribbed	65
Cereal bowl, 6-3/8" d	30
Comport, 7" d, cov	60

Item	Pink
Comport, 9" d	950
Console bowl, 10-1/2" d, three legs	325
Cookie jar, cov	110
Creamer	40
Cup	40
Flower bowl, crystal frog	50
Plate, 7-1/4" d, salad	35
Plate, 8-1/4" d, luncheon	32
Plate, 10-1/2" d, dinner	40
Plate, 10-1/2" d, grill	28.50
Plate, 13" d, four parts, solid lace	65
Plate, 13" d, solid lace	65
Platter, 12-3/4" l	48
Platter, 12-3/4" l, five parts	42
Relish dish, 7-1/2" d, three parts, deep	60

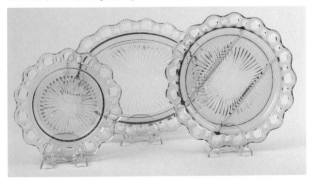

Old Colony Lace Edge, pink luncheon plate
$32, platter $48, and divided relish $60.

Item	Pink
Relish plate, 10-1/2" d, three parts	35
Salad bowl, 7-3/4" d, ribbed	60
Saucer	12
Sherbet, ftd	175
Sugar	25
Tumbler, 5 oz, 3-1/2" h, flat	120
Tumbler, 9 oz, 4-1/2" h, flat	32.50
Tumbler, 10-1/2 oz, 5" h, ftd	95
Vase, 7" h	650

Old Colony Lace Edge, pink satin-finish candlestick $350 pair.

OLD ENGLISH

Swatches

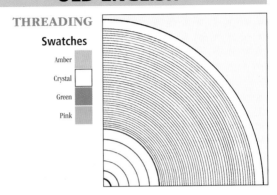

Amber

Crystal

Green

Pink

Manufactured by Indiana Glass Company, Dunkirk, Ind., late 1920s. Made in amber, crystal, green, and pink.

Item	Amber	Crystal	Green	Pink
Bowl, 4" d, flat	$20	$18	$22	$20
Bowl, 9-1/2" d, flat	35	25	35	35
Candlesticks, pr, 4" h	35	25	45	35
Candy dish, cov, flat	50	40	50	50
Candy jar, cov	55	45	55	55
Cheese compote, 3-1/2" h	17.50	12	17.50	17.50
Cheese plate, indent	20	10	20	20
Compote, 3-1/2" h, 6-3/8" w, two handles	24	12	24	24
Compote, 3-1/2" h, 7" w	24	12	24	24
Creamer	18	10	18	18
Egg cup	-	10	-	-

Item	Amber	Crystal	Green	Pink
Fruit bowl, 9" d, ftd	30	20	30	30
Fruit stand, 11" h, ftd	50	18	40	40
Goblet, 8 oz, 5-3/4" h	30	15	30	30
Pitcher	70	35	70	70
Pitcher, cov	125	55	125	125
Sandwich server, center handle	60	-	60	60
Sherbet	20	10	20	20
Sugar, cov	38	14	38	38
Tumbler, 4-1/2" h, ftd	24	12	32.50	28
Tumbler, 5-1/2" h, ftd	40	20	40	65
Vase, 5-3/8" h, 7" w, fan-shape	48	24	48	48
Vase, 8" h, 4-1/2" w, ftd	45	20	45	45
Vase, 8-1/4" h, 4-1/4" w, ftd	45	20	45	45
Vase, 12" h, ftd	72	35	72	72

Old English, green compote $24.

OVIDE

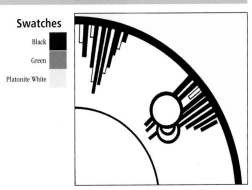

Swatches

Black

Green

Platonite White

Manufactured by Hazel Atlas Glass Company, Clarksburg, W.V., and Zanesville, Ohio, 1930-35 and in the 1950s.

Made in black, green, and Platonite white with fired-on colors in the 1950s.

Item	Black	Green	Platonite
Berry bowl, 4-3/4" d	$-	$5.50	$6
Berry bowl, 8" d	-	-	22
Candy dish, cov	50	24	35
Cereal bowl, 5-1/2" d	10	-	12.50
Creamer	10	6	18
Cup	8	4.50	5
Egg cup	-	-	22
Fruit cocktail, ftd	5	4.50	-
Plate, 6" d, sherbet	-	2.50	6
Plate, 8" d, luncheon	8	3.50	15

Ovide, green sugar $7, and green creamer $6.

Item	Black	Green	Platonite
Plate, 9" d, dinner	-	8	10
Platter, 11" d	-	-	24
Salt and pepper shakers, pr	32	28	25
Saucer	4.50	2.50	3
Sherbet	6.50	3.50	5
Sugar, open	10	7	20
Tumbler	18	-	14

Ovide, pink and gray platonite luncheon plate $15.

OYSTER & PEARL

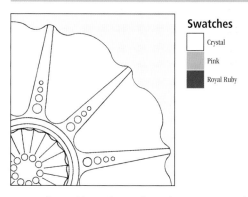

Swatches

☐ Crystal

☐ Pink

☐ Royal Ruby

Manufactured by Anchor Hocking Glass Corporation, from 1938 to 1940.

Made in crystal, pink, royal ruby, and white with fired-on green or pink.

Item	Crystal	Pink	Royal Ruby	White, Fired-On Green	White, Fired-On Pink
Bowl, 5-1/2" d, handle	$8	$15	$20	$-	$-
Bowl, 5-1/4" w, handle, heart-shape	15	21	-	20	15
Bowl, 6-1/2" d, handle	12	15	28	-	-
Candleholders, pr, 3-1/2" h	35	45	65	25	25
Fruit bowl, 10-1/2" d, deep	20	25	50	30	30

Oyster and Pearl, royal ruby candlestick $32.50, and pink candlestick $22.50.

Oyster and Pearl, 10-1/2" pink fruit bowl $25.

Item	Crystal	Pink	Royal Ruby	White, Fired-On Green	White, Fired-On Pink
Relish dish, 10-1/4" l, divided	10	35	-	-	-
Sandwich plate, 13-1/2" d	20	40	50	-	-

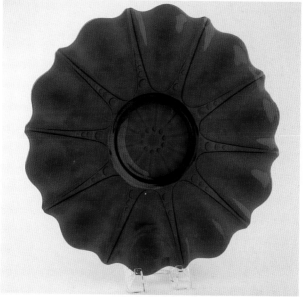

Oyster and Pearl, ruby sandwich plate $50.

PARK AVENUE

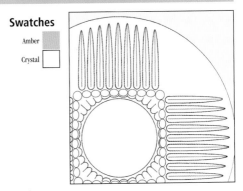

Swatches

Amber

Crystal

Manufactured by Federal Glass Company, Columbus, Ohio, 1941 to the early 1970s.

Made in amber, crystal, and crystal with gold trim. Values for crystal and crystal with gold trim are the same.

Item	Amber	Crystal
Ashtray, 3-1/2" sq	$-	$5
Ashtray, 4-1/2" sq	-	6.50
Candleholder, pr, 5" d	-	10
Dessert bowl, 5" d	8.50	5
Iced tea tumbler, 12 oz	12	6.50
Juice tumbler, 4-1/2 oz	5	5
Tumbler, 9 oz	7.50	5.50
Tumbler, 10 oz	9	6
Vegetable bowl, 8-1/2" d	18	10
Whiskey tumbler, 1-1/4 oz	-	4.50

Park Avenue, juice tumbler, crystal with gold band $5.

PARROT

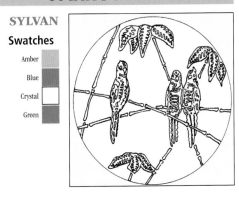

Manufactured by Federal Glass Company, Columbus, Ohio, from 1931 to 1932.

Made in amber and green, with limited production in blue and crystal.

Item	Amber	Green
Berry bowl, 8" d	$75	$80
Butter dish, cov	1,250	475
Creamer, ftd	65	55
Cup	35	40
Hot plate, 5" d, pointed	875	900
Hot plate, round	-	950
Pitcher, 80 oz, 8-1/2" h	-	2,500
Plate, 5-3/4" d, sherbet	45	35
Plate, 7-1/2" d, salad	-	60
Plate, 9" d, dinner	50	95

Item	Amber	Green
Plate, 10-1/2" d, grill, round	35	-
Plate, 10-1/2" d, grill, square	-	60
Platter, 11-1/4" l, oblong	65	70
Salt and pepper shakers, pr	-	270
Saucer	18	18
Sherbet, ftd, cone	22.50	27.50
Sugar, cov	450	320
Tumbler, 10 oz, 4-1/4" h	100	130
Tumbler, 10 oz, 5-1/2" h, ftd, Madrid mold	145	-
Tumbler, 12 oz, 5-1/2" h	115	160
Tumbler, 5-3/4" h, ftd, heavy	100	120
Vegetable bowl, 10" l, oval	75	65

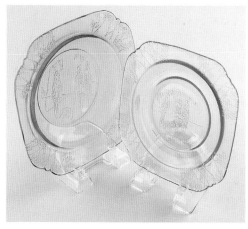

Parrot, amber jam dish $75, and green sherbet plate $35.

PATRICIAN

SPOKE

Swatches

Amber

Crystal

Green

Pink

Manufactured by Federal Glass Company, Columbus, Ohio, from 1933 to 1937.

Made in amber (also called Golden Glo), crystal, green, and pink.

Item	Amber	Crystal	Green	Pink
Berry bowl, 5" d	$12.50	$10	$12.50	$18.50
Berry bowl, 8-1/2" d	35	15	37.50	35
Butter dish, cov	100	100	215	225
Cereal bowl, 6" d	30	27.50	27.50	25
Cookie jar, cov	75	80	500	-
Cream soup, 4-3/4" d	28	25	24.50	26.50
Creamer, ftd	12.50	9.50	12.50	12.50
Cup	12	12	15	18.50
Pitcher, 75 oz, 8" h, molded handle	120	125	125	115
Pitcher, 75 oz, 8-1/4" h, applied handle	150	140	150	145
Plate, 6" d, sherbet	10	8.50	10	10

Patrician, 5-1/4" amber footed tumbler $50.

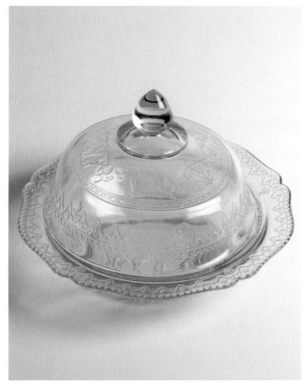

Patrician, amber covered butter, $100.

Item	Amber	Crystal	Green	Pink
Plate, 7-1/2" d, salad	18	15	20	15
Plate, 9" d, luncheon	15	12.50	12	22.50
Plate, 10-1/2 d, dinner	12.50	12.75	32	36
Platter, 11-1/2" l, oval	35	30	30	28
Salt and pepper shakers, pr	65	65	65	85
Saucer	10	9.25	9.50	12.50
Sherbet	15	12	14	16
Sugar	12.50	9	18.50	12.50
Tumbler, 8 oz, 5-1/4" h, ftd	50	42	50	-
Tumbler, 14 oz, 5-1/2" h	42	38	40	46
Vegetable bowl, 10" l, oval	35	30	38.50	30

Patrician, amber cream soup bowl $28, sherbet $15, and cup $12.50.

PATRICK

Swatches

Pink

Yellow

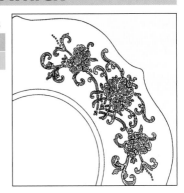

Manufactured by Lancaster Glass Company, Lancaster, Ohio, early 1930s.

Made in pink and yellow.

Item	Pink	Yellow
Candlesticks, pr	**$200**	**$160**
Candy dish, three ftd	175	175
Cheese and cracker set	150	130
Cocktail, 4" h	85	85
Console bowl, 11" d	150	150
Creamer	90	40
Cup	85	40
Fruit bowl, 9" d, handle	175	130
Goblet, 10 oz, 6" h	85	75
Juice goblet, 6 oz, 4-3/4" h	85	75
Mayonnaise, three pieces	200	140

Item	Pink	Yellow
Plate, 7" d, sherbet	20	15
Plate, 7-1/2" d, salad	25	20
Plate, 8" d, luncheon	45	30
Saucer	20	12
Sherbet, 4-3/4" d	72	60
Sugar	90	40
Tray, 11" d, center handle	165	120
Tray, 11" d, two handles	80	65

Patrick, yellow tray with caned center $65.

PETALWARE

Swatches

Cobalt Blue

Cremax

Crystal

Monax, Plain

Pink

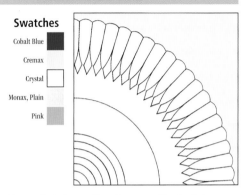

Manufactured by Macbeth-Evans Glass Company, Charleroi, Pa., from 1930 to 1940.

Made in cobalt blue, Cremax, crystal, fired-on red, blue, green and yellow, Monax and pink. Florette is the name given to a floral decorated with a pointed petal. There are other patterns, such as red flower with a red rim, fruit and other floral patterns.

Crystal values are approximately 50 percent less than those listed for Cremax. Cobalt blue production was limited and the mustard is currently valued at $15 when complete with its metal lid. Monax Regency is priced the same as Monax Florette.

Item	Cremax	Cremax, Gold Trim	Fired-On Colors
Berry bowl, 9" d	$30	$32	$-
Cereal bowl, 5-1/4" d	15	17.50	8.50

Petalware, pink dinner plate $20, creamer $15, and sugar $12.

Item	Cremax	Cremax, Gold Trim	Fired-On Colors
Cream soup liner	-	-	-
Cream soup, 4-1/2" d	12.50	12	12
Creamer, ftd	12.50	15	8.50
Cup	8	10	9.50
Lamp shade, 9" d	16.50	-	-
Plate, 6" d, sherbet	4.50	50	6
Plate, 8" d, salad	12	8	7.50
Plate, 9" d, dinner	25	14	8.50
Platter, 13" l, oval	25	20	20
Saucer	3.50	3	4
Sherbet, 4" h, low ftd	-	-	-
Sherbet, 4-1/2" h, low ftd	15	12	8
Soup bowl, 7" d	65	60	70
Sugar, ftd	7.50	11	12
Tumbler, 12 oz, 4-5/8" h	-	-	-

Petalware, 13" pink oval platter $17.50.

Item	Monax, Florette	Monax, Plain	Pink
Berry bowl, 9" d	**$35.50**	**$18**	**$25**
Cereal bowl, 5-1/4" d	15.50	9	15
Cream soup liner	-	18.75	-
Cream soup, 4-1/2" d	15	10	19
Creamer, ftd	15	12	15
Cup	12	6.50	6
Lamp shade, 9" d	14	18	-
Plate, 6" d, sherbet	6	2.50	4.50
Plate, 8" d, salad	15	4.50	10
Plate, 9" d, dinner	16.50	9	20
Platter, 13" l, oval	25	20	17.50
Saucer	5	3.50	5
Sherbet, 4" h, low ftd	-	32	-
Sherbet, 4-1/2" h, low ftd	12	10	8.50
Soup bowl, 7" d	65	60	-
Sugar, ftd	15	10	12
Tumbler, 12 oz, 4-5/8" h	-	-	25

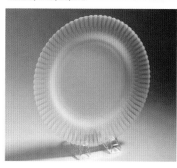

Petalware, Monax dinner plate, $9.

PINEAPPLE & FLORAL

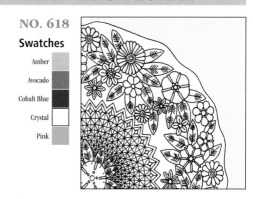

NO. 618

Swatches

Amber	
Avocado	
Cobalt Blue	
Crystal	
Pink	

Manufactured by Indiana Glass Company, Dunkirk, Ind., from 1932 to 1937, and 1960s to 1980s.

Made in amber, avocado (late 1960s), cobalt blue (1980s), crystal, fired-on green, fired-on red, and pink (1980s).

Reproductions: † Salad bowl and diamond-shaped comport have been reproduced in several different colors, including crystal, pink, and avocado green.

Item	Amber	Crystal	Fired-On Red
Ashtray, 4-1/2" d	$20	$16.50	$20
Berry bowl, 4-3/4" d	24	20	22
Cereal bowl, 6" d	24	30	22
Comport, diamond-shape	10	3.50	10
Creamer, diamond-shape	10	9.50	10

Item	Amber	Crystal	Fired-On Red
Cream soup	16.50	18	16.50
Cup	10	12	10
Plate, 6" d, sherbet	8	7.50	8
Plate, 8-3/8" d, salad	12	8	12
Plate, 9-3/8" d, dinner	17.50	18	17.50
Plate, 9-3/4" d, indentation	-	25	-
Plate, 11" d, closed handles	24	20	24
Plate, 11-1/2" d, indentation	-	25	-
Platter, 11" l, closed handles	20	8	20
Relish, 11-1/2" d, divided	28	20	28
Salad bowl, 7" d †	10	5	10
Sandwich plate, 11-1/2" d	24	20	24
Saucer	4.50	5	7.50
Sherbet, ftd	28	24	28
Sugar, diamond-shape	10	9.50	10

Pineapple & Floral, crystal sugar $9.50, and creamer $9.50.

Item	Amber	Crystal	Fired-On Red
Tumbler, 8 oz, 4-1/4" h	40	40	40
Tumbler, 12 oz, 5" h	48	46.50	48
Vase, cone shape	45	42.50	45
Vegetable bowl, 10" l, oval	32	30	32

Pineapple & Floral, amber cream soup $16.50.

Pineapple and Floral, 11-1/4" crystal two-handled, three-part divided relish $20.

PIONEER

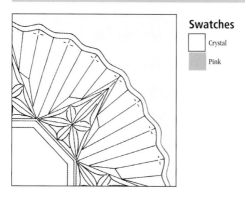

Swatches

☐ Crystal

▨ Pink

Manufactured by Federal Glass Co., Columbus, Ohio, starting in the 1940s.

Originally made in pink, crystal was added later. The crystal 11" fluted bowl and 12" dinner plate were made until 1973.

Item	Crystal	Pink
Bowl, 7" d, low, fruits center	$8	$10
Bowl, 7-3/4" d, ruffled, fruits center	10	12
Bowl, 10-1/2" d, fruits center	12	14
Bowl, 10-1/2" d, plain center	10	12
Bowl, 11" d, ruffled, fruits center	15	18
Bowl, 11" d, ruffled, plain center	12	15
Nappy, 5-3/8" d, fruits center	8	10
Nappy, 5-3/8" d, plain center	6	8
Plate, 8" d, luncheon, fruits center	6	8
Plate, 8" d, luncheon, plain center	6	8

Item	Crystal	Pink
Plate, 12" d, fruit center	10	12
Plate, 12" d, plain center	10	12

Pioneer, pink plate with fruit center $12.

PRETZEL

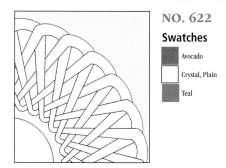

NO. 622

Swatches

■ Avocado

□ Crystal, Plain

■ Teal

Manufactured by Indiana Glass Company, Dunkirk, Ind., from late 1930s to 1960s.

Made in avocado, crystal, and teal. Some crystal pieces have a fruit decoration. Recent amber, blue, and opaque white issues. A teal cup and saucer is valued at $165.

Item	Crystal, Plain	Crystal, Fruits
Berry bowl, 9-3/8" d	$18	$-
Celery tray, 10-1/4" l	18	-
Creamer	10	-
Cup	6.50	-
Iced tea tumbler, 12 oz, 5-1/2" h	90	-
Juice tumbler	35	-
Pitcher, 39 oz	250	-
Plate, 6" d	3.50	5
Plate, 6" d, tab handle	7	-

Item	Crystal, Plain	Crystal, Fruits
Plate, 7-1/4" w, sq, indent	8	-
Plate, 7-1/4" w, sq, indent, three parts	12	-
Plate, 8-3/8" d, salad	8.50	4
Plate, 9-3/8" d, dinner	10	20
Plate, 10" d, dinner	12	15
Relish, 7", three parts	10	-
Sandwich plate, 11-1/2" d	12.50	12
Saucer	2	4
Sugar	10	-
Tumbler, 5 oz, 3-1/2" h	50	-
Tumbler, 9 oz, 4-1/2" h	70	-

Pretzel, crystal sugar $10, and creamer $10.

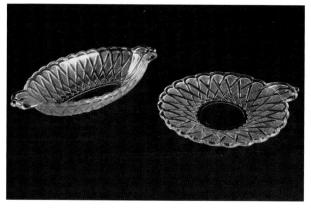

Pretzel, crystal two-handled oval celery tray
$18, and 6" crystal tab-handled plate $7.

PRIMO

PANELED ASTER

Swatches

Green

Yellow

Manufactured by U.S. Glass Company, Pittsburgh, Pa., early 1930s. Made in green and yellow.

Item	Green	Yellow
Bowl, 4-1/2" d	$20	$25
Bowl, 7-3/4" d	38	40
Cake plate, 10" d, 3 ftd	40	45
Coaster/ashtray	8.75	8.75
Creamer	12	15
Cup	14.50	15
Hostess tray, 5-3/4" d, handles	42	45
Plate, 7-1/2" d	10.25	12
Plate, 10" d, dinner	27.50	30
Plate, 10" d, grill	18	22.50
Saucer	3.25	5
Sherbet	14.25	14.50
Sugar	12	12
Tumbler, 9 oz, 5-3/4" h, ftd	25	30

Primo, yellow cup $14.50.

PRINCESS

Swatches

Blue

Green

Pink

Topaz Yellow

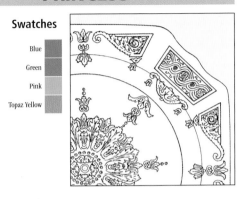

Manufactured by Hocking Glass Company, Lancaster, Ohio, from 1931 to 1935.

Made in apricot yellow, blue, green, pink, and topaz yellow.

Reproductions: † The candy dish and salt and pepper shakers have been reproduced in blue, green and pink.

Item	Apricot Yellow	Blue	Green	Pink	Topaz Yellow
Ashtray, 4-1/2" d	**$110**	**$-**	**$72**	**$90**	**$110**
Berry bowl, 4-1/2" d	55	-	40	32	55
Butter dish, cov	700	-	115	120	700
Cake plate, 10" d, ftd	-	-	40	100	-
Candy dish, cov †	-	-	75	95	-
Cereal bowl, 5" d	-	-	50	45	-
Coaster	100	-	85	65	100
Cookie jar, cov	-	875	85	75	

Princess, green covered candy $75.

Item	Apricot Yellow	Blue	Green	Pink	Topaz Yellow
Creamer, oval	25	-	15	17.50	22.50
Cup	10	120	15	17.50	15
Hat-shaped bowl, 9-1/2" d	125	-	80	50	125
Iced tea tumbler, 13 oz, 5-1/2" h	45	-	125	115	30
Juice tumbler, 5 oz, 3" h	28	-	25	28	30
Pitcher, 37 oz, 6" h	775	-	60	75	775
Plate, 8" d, salad	15	-	20	15	20
Plate, 9-1/2" d, dinner	25	-	30	35	30
Plate, 9-1/2" d, grill	10	175	20	15	10
Plate, 10-1/2" d, grill, closed handles	10	-	15	15	10
Platter, 12" l, closed handles	60	-	25	25	60
Relish, 7-1/2" l, divided, four parts	100	-	35	30	100
Relish, 7-1/2" l, plain	225	-	195	195	225
Salad bowl, 9" d, octagonal	125	-	55	40	125
Salt and pepper shakers, pr, 4-1/2" h †	75	-	60	65	85
Sandwich plate, 10-1/4" d, closed handles	175	-	30	35	175
Saucer, 6" sq	2.75	65	14.50	10	3.75
Sherbet, ftd	40	-	25	25	40
Spice shakers, pr, 5-1/2" h	-	-	20	-	-
Sugar, cov	30	-	35	65	30
Tumbler, 9 oz, 4" h	25	-	28	25	25
Tumbler, 9 oz, 4-3/4" h, sq, ftd	-	-	65	25	-

Item	Apricot Yellow	Blue	Green	Pink	Topaz Yellow
Tumbler, 12-1/2 oz, 6-1/2" h, ftd	25	-	180	95	25
Vase, 8" h	-	-	65	75	-
Vegetable bowl, 10" l, oval	60	-	50	50	65

Princess, green cookie jar $85.

PYRAMID

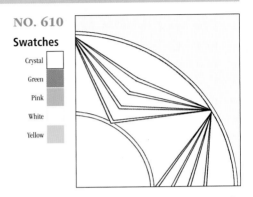

NO. 610

Swatches

Crystal
Green
Pink
White
Yellow

Manufactured by Indiana Glass Company, Dunkirk, Ind., from 1926 to 1932.

Made in crystal, green, pink, white, and yellow. Later production in 1974 to 1975 by Tiara produced black and blue pieces. Prices for black not firmly established in secondary market at this time.

Item	Crystal	Green	Pink	Yellow
Berry bowl, 4-3/4" d	$20	$35	$35	$65
Berry bowl, 8-1/2" d	30	65	55	75
Bowl, 9-1/2" l, oval	50	45	40	65
Creamer	20	35	35	40
Ice tub	95	145	155	225
Pickle dish, 9-1/2" l, 5-3/4" w	30	35	35	65
Pitcher	395	265	400	550
Relish, four parts, handles	25	65	60	70

Item	Crystal	Green	Pink	Yellow
Sugar	20	35	35	40
Tray for creamer and sugar	25	30	30	35
Tumbler, 8 oz, ftd	55	50	55	75
Tumbler, 11 oz, ftd	70	75	50	95

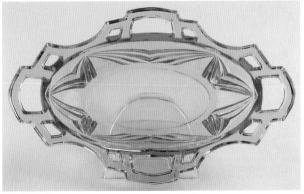

Pyramid, green pickle dish $35.

QUEEN MARY

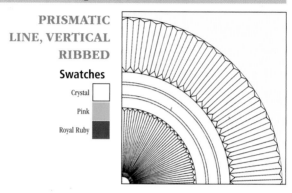

PRISMATIC LINE, VERTICAL RIBBED

Swatches

Crystal	
Pink	
Royal Ruby	

Manufactured by Hocking Glass Company, Lancaster, Ohio, from 1936 to 1948.

Made in crystal, pink, and Royal Ruby.

Item	Crystal	Pink	Royal Ruby
Ashtray, 2" x 3-3/4" l, oval	$5	$5.50	$5
Ashtray, 3-1/2" d, round	4	-	-
Berry bowl, 4-1/2" d	3	8	-
Berry bowl, 5" d	5	15	-
Berry bowl, 8-3/4" d	10	17.50	-
Bowl, 4" d, one handle	4	7.50	-
Bowl, 5-1/2" d, two handles	8	15	-
Bowl, 7" d	7.50	35	-
Butter dish, cov	42	125	-
Candlesticks, pr, two lite, 4-1/2" h	30	-	70

Queen Mary, pink oval open sugar, $24, and oval creamer, $12.

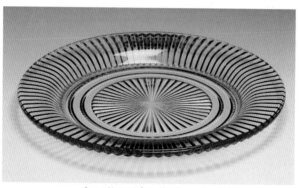

Queen Mary, pink, 9-1/2" dinner plate, $65.

Item	Crystal	Pink	Royal Ruby
Candy dish, cov	70	42	-
Celery tray, 5" x 10"	10	24	-
Cereal bowl, 6" d	8	30	-
Cigarette jar, 2" x 3" oval	6.50	7.50	-
Coaster, 3-1/2" d	4	5	-
Coaster/ashtray, 4-1/4" sq	4	6	-
Comport, 5-3/4"	9	14	-
Creamer, ftd	8	40	-
Creamer, oval	8	12	-
Cup, large	6	9.50	-
Cup, small	8	12	-
Juice tumbler, 5 oz, 3-1/2" h	9.50	18	-
Pickle dish, 5" x 10"	10	24	-
Plate, 6" d, sherbet	4	10	-
Plate, 6-1/2" d, bread and butter	6	-	-
Plate, 8-1/4" d, salad	6	-	-
Plate, 9-1/2" d, dinner	35	65	-
Preserve, cov	30	125	-
Relish, clover-shape	15	17.50	-
Relish, 12" d, three parts	10	15	-
Relish, 14" d, four parts	15	17.50	-
Salt and pepper shakers, pr	30	-	-
Sandwich plate, 12" d	20	17.50	-
Saucer	2	5	-
Serving tray, 14" d	15	9	-
Sherbet, ftd	6	15	-
Sugar, ftd	-	40	-
Sugar, oval	8	24	-
Tumbler, 9 oz, 4" h	6	17.50	-
Tumbler, 10 oz, 5" h, ftd	35	70	-

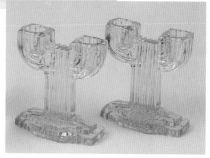

Queen Mary, crystal bowl
$7.50, and candlesticks
$30 pair.

RAINDROPS

Swatches

Crystal

Green

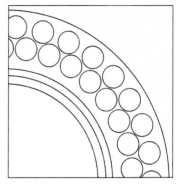

Manufactured by Federal Glass Company, Columbus, Ohio, from 1929 to 1933.

Made in crystal and green.

Item	Crystal	Green
Berry bowl, 7-1/2" d	$30	$45
Cereal bowl, 6" d	10	15
Creamer	8	10
Cup	8.50	8.50
Fruit bowl, 4-1/2" d	5	12
Plate, 6" d, sherbet	1.50	3
Plate, 8" d, luncheon	4	7.50
Salt and pepper shakers, pr	200	350
Saucer	3	4.50
Sherbet	4.50	7.50
Sugar, cov	7.50	15

Raindrops, green creamer, $10, and open sugar, $12.

Raindrops, 4-1/2" green fruit bowl, $12.

Item	Crystal	Green
Tumbler, 4 oz, 3" h	4	7
Tumbler, 5 oz, 3-7/8" h	5.50	9.50
Tumbler, 9-1/2 oz, 4-1/8" h	6	12
Tumblers, 10 oz, 5" h	6	12
Tumblers, 14 oz, 5-3/8" h	7.50	15
Whiskey, 1 oz, 1-7/8" h	7.50	10

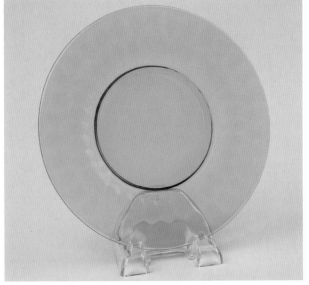

Raindrops, green luncheon plate $7.50.

RIBBON

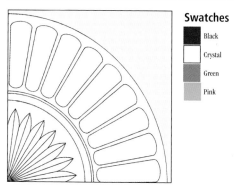

Swatches

- Black
- Crystal
- Green
- Pink

Manufactured by Hazel Atlas Glass Company, Clarksburg, W.V., and Zanesville, Ohio, early 1930s.

Made in black, crystal, green, and pink. Production in pink was limited to salt and pepper shakers, valued at $40.

Item	Black	Crystal	Green
Berry bowl, 4" d	$-	$20	$22
Berry bowl, 8" d	-	27.50	45
Bowl, 9" d, wide bands	-	-	35
Candy dish, cov	45	35	45
Cereal bowl, 5" d	-	20	25
Creamer, ftd	-	10	18
Cup	-	4.50	6.50
Plate, 6-1/4" d, sherbet	-	3.50	4.50
Plate, 8" d, luncheon	15	7	10

Item	Black	Crystal	Green
Salt and pepper shakers, pr	45	36	32
Saucer	-	2	3.50
Sherbet	-	6	8
Sugar, ftd	-	12	18.50
Tumbler, 10 oz, 6" h	-	28	30

Ribbon, green cup $6.50, and creamer $18.

RING

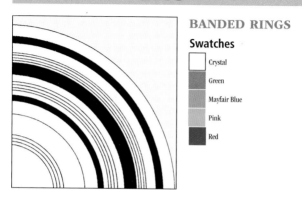

Manufactured by Hocking Glass Company, Lancaster, Ohio, from 1927 to 1933.

Made in crystal, crystal with rings of black, blue, pink, red, orange, silver, and yellow; and green, Mayfair blue, pink, and red. Prices for decorated pieces are quite similar to each other.

Item	Crystal	Decorated	Green
Berry bowl, 5" d	$4	$9	$6
Berry bowl, 8" d	7.50	16	16
Bowl, 5-1/4" d, divided	12.50	-	-
Butter tub	24	25	20
Cereal bowl	-	5	8
Cocktail shaker	20	30	27.50
Cocktail, 3-1/2 oz, 3-3/4" h	12	18	18
Creamer, ftd	5	10	10
Cup	5	6	5

Item	Crystal	Decorated	Green
Decanter, stopper	30	35	32
Ice bucket	24	33	30
Ice tub	24	25	20
Iced tea tumbler, 6-1/2" h	10	15	15
Juice tumbler, 3-1/2" h, ftd	6.50	10	15
Old fashioned tumbler, 8 oz, 4" h	15	17.50	17.50
Pitcher, 60 oz, 8" h	15	25	25
Pitcher, 80 oz, 8-1/2" h	20	35	36
Plate, 6-1/2" d, off-center ring	5.50	6.50	8
Plate, 6-1/4" d, sherbet	3.25	6.50	4
Plate, 8" d, luncheon	3	6	9
Salt and pepper shakers, pr, 3" h	20	40	42
Sandwich plate, 11-3/4" d	9.50	15	15
Sandwich server, center handle	15	27.50	27.50
Saucer	1.50	4	2.50
Sherbet, 4-3/4" h	6.50	10	12

Ring, green ice tub $20.

Ring, green footed wine, $24, and 4-3/4" green flat tumbler, $9.

Item	Crystal	Decorated	Green
Sherbet, flat, 6-1/2" d underplate	12	18	21
Soup bowl, 7" d	10	9	8
Sugar, ftd	5	10	3
Tumbler, 4 oz, 3" h	4	6.50	6
Tumbler, 5-1/2" h, ftd	6	10	10
Tumbler, 5 oz, 3-1/2" h	5	6.50	12
Tumbler, 9 oz, 4-1/4" h	4.50	18	9
Tumbler, 10 oz, 4-3/4" h	8.50	-	9
Tumbler, 12 oz, 5-1/8" h, ftd	10	12	20
Vase, 8" h	20	35	37.50
Whiskey, 1-1/2 oz, 2" h	8.50	10	12
Wine, 3-1/2 oz, 4-1/2" h	17.50	20	24

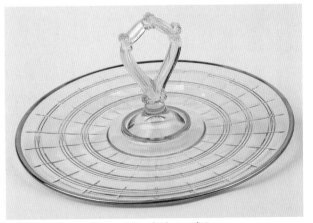

Ring, crystal sandwich server $15.

ROSE CAMEO

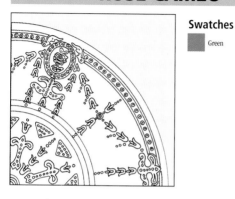

Swatches

Green

Manufactured by Belmont Tumbler Company, Bellaire, Ohio, in 1931. Made in green.

Item	Green
Berry bowl, 4-1/2" d	$15
Cereal bowl, 5" d	27.50
Bowl, 6" d, straight sides	30
Plate, 7" d, salad	16
Sherbet	15
Tumbler, 5" h, ftd	28
Tumbler, 5" h, ftd, sterling silver trim	30

Rose Cameo, green tumbler $28.

ROSEMARY

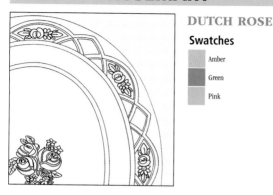

DUTCH ROSE

Swatches

Amber

Green

Pink

Manufactured by Federal Glass Company, Columbus, Ohio, from 1935 to 1937.

Made in amber, green, and pink.

Item	Amber	Green	Pink
Berry bowl, 5" d	$7	$17.50	$17.50
Cereal bowl, 6" d	30	32	35
Cream soup, 5" d	20	25	30
Creamer, ftd	15	16	20
Cup	7.50	12.50	15
Plate, 6-3/4" d, salad	6.25	12	12.50
Plate, 9-1/2" d, dinner	10	15	30
Plate, 9-1/2" d, grill	12	15	22
Platter, 12" l, oval	18	24	35
Saucer	4.50	8.50	9.50

Item	Amber	Green	Pink
Sugar, ftd	15	16	20
Tumbler, 9 oz, 4-1/4" h	35	38	50
Vegetable bowl, 10" l, oval	17.50	40	45

Rosemary, green platter $24.

ROULETTE

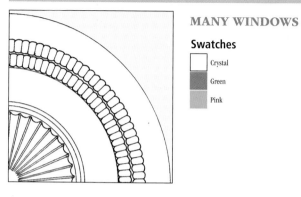

MANY WINDOWS

Swatches

☐	Crystal
■	Green
■	Pink

Manufactured by Hocking Glass Company, Lancaster, Ohio, from 1935 to 1939.

Made in crystal, green, and pink.

Item	Crystal	Green	Pink
Cup	**$35**	**$8.50**	**$8.50**
Fruit bowl, 9" d	12	25	25
Iced tea tumbler, 12 oz, 5-1/8" h	24	40	35
Juice tumbler, 5 oz, 3-1/4" h	10	60	24
Old fashioned tumbler, 7-1/2 oz, 3-1/4" h	24	40	40
Pitcher, 65 oz, 8" h	30	35	45
Plate, 6" d, sherbet	3.50	4.50	5
Plate, 8-1/2" d, luncheon	7	8	6
Sandwich plate, 12" d	15	18.50	20
Saucer	2.50	4.50	3
Sherbet	8	10	12

*Roulette, 4-1/8" green flat tumbler, **$20**, and
5-1/2" green footed cone-shaped tumbler, **$30**.*

Item	Crystal	Green	Pink
Tumbler, 9 oz, 4-1/8" h	15	20	30
Tumbler, 10 oz, 5-1/2" h, ftd	18	30	35
Whiskey, 1-1/2 oz, 2-1/2" h	10	18	17.50

Roulette, green luncheon plate $8, and sherbet $10.

ROUND ROBIN

Swatches

Crystal

Iridescent

Green

Unknown maker, early 1930s.

Made in crystal, iridescent, and green. Crystal, produced as the base for iridescent pieces, is found occasionally.

Item	Iridescent	Green
Berry bowl, 4" d	$12	$10
Creamer, ftd	7.50	12
Cup	7.50	6
Domino tray	-	120
Plate, 6" d, sherbet	4	6
Plate, 8" d, luncheon	12	17.50
Sandwich plate, 12" d	15	17.50
Saucer	2.50	2
Sherbet	8.50	10
Sugar	7.50	12

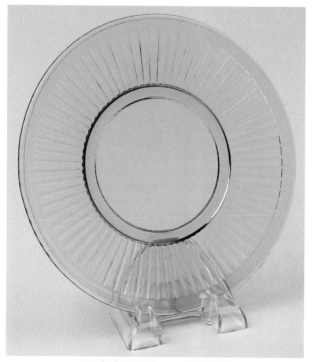

Round Robin, green luncheon plate $17.50.

ROXANA

Swatches

Crystal

Golden Topaz

White

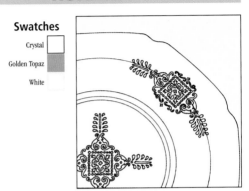

Manufactured by Hazel Atlas Glass Company, Clarksburg, W.V., and Zanesville, Ohio, in 1932.

Made in crystal, golden topaz, and white. Production in white was limited to a 4-1/2" bowl, valued at $15.

Item	Crystal	Golden Topaz
Berry bowl, 5" d	**$8.50**	**$15**
Bowl, 4-1/2" x 2-3/8"	8	15
Cereal bowl, 6" d	9	20
Plate, 5-1/2" d	5	12
Plate, 6" d, sherbet	5	10
Sherbet, ftd	8	12
Tumbler, 9 oz, 4-1/4" h	12	25

Roxana, 5-1/2" d golden topaz plate $12.

ROYAL LACE

Swatches

Amethyst
Cobalt Blue
Crystal
Green
Pink

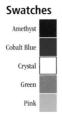

Manufactured by Hazel Atlas Glass Company, Clarksburg, W.V., and Zanesville, Ohio, from 1934 to 1941.

Made in cobalt (Ritz) blue, crystal, green, pink, and some amethyst.

Reproductions: † Reproductions include a 5 oz, 3-1/2" h tumbler, found in a darker cobalt blue. A cookie jar has also been reproduced in cobalt blue.

Item	Cobalt Blue	Crystal	Green	Pink
Berry bowl, 5" d	$50	$18	$65	$90
Berry bowl, 10" d	90	20	35	60
Bowl, 10" d, three legs, rolled edge	650	225	125	200
Bowl, 10" d, three legs, ruffled edge	750	95	125	165
Bowl, 10" d, three legs, straight edge	-	24	75	65
Butter dish, cov	865	90	275	200
Candlesticks, pr, rolled edge	-	45	85	60

Item	Cobalt Blue	Crystal	Green	Pink
Candlesticks, pr, ruffled edge	-	28	70	60
Candlesticks, pr, straight edge	-	35	75	55
Cookie jar, cov †	400	30	75	100

Royal Lace, crystal dinner plate $25.

Item	Cobalt Blue	Crystal	Green	Pink
Cream soup, 4-3/4" d	50	18	35	30
Creamer, ftd	65	15	25	20
Cup and saucer	60	16	35	32
Nut bowl	1,500	275	425	425
Pitcher, 48 oz, straight sides	225	45	110	85
Pitcher, 64 oz, 8" h	295	45	120	125
Pitcher, 68 oz, 8" h ice lip	320	60	-	115
Pitcher, 86 oz, 8" h	-	60	135	135
Pitcher, 96 oz, 9-1/2" h, ice lip	495	115	160	155
Plate, 6" d, sherbet	20	8.50	15	18
Plate, 8-1/2" d, luncheon	60	12	18	24
Plate, 9-7/8" d, dinner	55	25	45	40
Plate, 9-7/8" d, grill	40	20	25	22.50
Platter, 13" l, oval	60	30	45	48
Salt and pepper shakers, pr	395	65	130	85
Sherbet, ftd	50	18	60	35
Sherbet, metal holder	45	18	-	-
Sugar, cov	275	90	40	50
Sugar, open	-	15	25	20
Toddy or cider set	295	-	-	-
Tumbler, 5 oz, 3-1/2" h †	65	15	60	35
Tumbler, 9 oz, 4-1/8" h †	60	18	35	30
Tumbler, 10 oz, 4-7/8" h	245	25	60	60
Tumbler, 12 oz, 5-3/8" h	165	25	50	55
Vegetable bowl, 11" l, oval	60	25	35	95

ROYAL RUBY

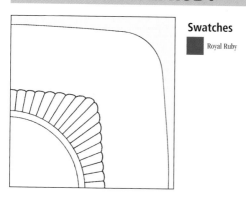

Swatches

■ Royal Ruby

Manufactured by Anchor Hocking Glass Corporation, Lancaster, Pa., from 1938 to 1967.

Made only in Royal Ruby.

Item	Royal Ruby
Apothecary jar, 8-1/2" h	$22
Ashtray, 4-1/2", leaf	5
Ashtray, 5-7/8", sq	7.50
Ashtray, 7-3/4"	32
Beer bottle, 7 oz	42.50
Beer bottle, 12 oz	32
Beer bottle, 16 oz	35
Beer bottle, 32 oz	40
Berry bowl, 4-5/8" d, small, square	9.50
Berry bowl, 8-1/2" d, round	25
Bonbon, 6-1/2" d	20

Item	Royal Ruby
Bowl, 7-3/8" w, sq	18.50
Bowl, 11" d, Rachael	50
Bowl, 12" l, oval, Rachael	70
Cereal bowl, 5-1/4" d	12
Cigarette box, card holder, 6-1/8" x 4"	90
Cocktail, 3-1/2 oz, Boopie	8.50
Cocktail, 3-1/2 oz, tumbler	10
Cordial, ftd	15
Creamer, flat	8
Creamer, ftd	10
Cup, round	12
Cup, square	7.50
Dessert bowl, 4-3/4" w, sq	12
Fruit bowl, 4-1/4" d	10
Goblet, 9 oz	9
Goblet, 9-1/2 oz	14
Goblet, ball stem	15
Ice bucket	55
Iced tea goblet, 14 oz, Boopie	20
Iced tea tumbler, 13 oz, 6" h, ftd	14
Ivy ball, 4" h, Wilson	10
Juice tumbler, 4 oz	7
Juice tumbler, 5-1/2 oz	10
Juice tumbler, 5 oz, flat or ftd	8
Juice pitcher	40
Lamp	35
Marmalade, ruby top, crystal base	22
Pitcher, 3 qt, tilted	45
Pitcher, 3 qt, upright	38

Item	Royal Ruby
Pitcher, 42 oz, tilted	35
Pitcher, 42 oz, upright	40
Pitcher, 86 oz, 8-1/2"	35
Plate, 6-1/4" d, sherbet	6.50
Plate, 7" d, salad	5.50
Plate, 7-3/4" w, sq, salad	12.50
Plate, 8-3/8" w, sq, luncheon	12
Plate, 9-1/8" d, dinner	17.50
Plate, 13-3/4" d	35
Popcorn bowl, 5-1/4" d	12.50
Popcorn bowl, 10" d, deep	40
Puff box, ruby top, crystal base, orig label	28
Punch bowl and stand	75
Punch set, 14 pieces	200

*Royal Ruby, punch set (includes 14 pieces), punch bowl
and six cups are shown, value for entire set $200.*

Royal Ruby, sugar $8, creamer (on pedestal) $10,
square cup $7.50, and square saucer $4.

Royal Ruby, 5-1/2" tilted ball pitcher $45.

Item	Royal Ruby
Punch cup	3
Relish, 3-3/4" x 8-3/4", tab handle	16
Salad bowl, 8-1/2" d	19
Salad bowl, 11-1/2" d	48
Saucer, 5-3/8" w, sq	4
Saucer, round	4
Set, 50 pcs, orig labels, orig box	350
Sherbet, 6-1/2 oz, stemmed	9.50
Sherbet, 6 oz, Boopie	9
Shot glass	4.50
Soup bowl, 7-1/2" d	13
Sugar, flat	8
Sugar, footed	8
Sugar lid, notched	11
Tray, center handle, ruffled	16.50
Tumbler, 5 oz, 3-1/2" h	15
Tumbler, 9 oz, Windsor	8
Tumbler, 10 oz, 5" h, ftd	15
Tumbler, 14 oz, 5" h	9
Tumbler, 15 oz, long boy	15
Vase, 3-3/4" h, Roosevelt	7.50
Vase, 4" h, Wilson, fancy edge	8
Vase, 6-3/8" h, Harding	9
Vase, 6-5/8" h, Coolidge	20
Vase, 9" h, Hoover, plain	20
Vase, 9" h, Hoover, white birds on branch dec	25
Vase, 10" h, fluted, star base	35
Vase, 10" h, ftd, Rachael	50
Vegetable bowl, 8" l, oval	30
Wine, 2-1/2 oz, ftd	12.50

S-PATTERN

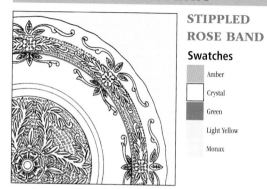

STIPPLED ROSE BAND

Swatches

	Amber
	Crystal
	Green
	Light Yellow
	Monax

Manufactured by Macbeth-Evans Glass Company, Charleroi, Pa., from 1930 to 1933.

Made in amber, crystal, crystal with amber, blue, green, pink or silver trims, fired-on red, green, light yellow and Monax.

Item	Amber	Crystal	Crystal with Trims
Berry bowl, 8-1/2" d	$8.50	$12	$-
Cake plate, 11-3/4" d	50	48	55
Cake plate, 13" d	80	65	75
Cereal bowl, 5-1/2" d	9.50	4.50	6.50
Creamer, thick	7.50	6.50	6
Creamer, thin	7.50	6.50	6
Cup, thick	5	4	5.50
Cup, thin	5	4	5.50
Pitcher, 80 oz	-	75	-

Item	Amber	Crystal	Crystal with Trims
Plate, 6" d, sherbet	3.50	3	4
Plate, 8-1/4" d, luncheon	8	7.50	9.50
Plate, 9-1/4" d, dinner	9.50	-	12.50
Plate, grill	8.50	6.50	9
Saucer	4	3	4
Sherbet, low, ftd	8	5.50	8.50
Sugar, thick	7.50	6.50	6
Sugar, thin	7.50	6.50	6
Tumbler, 5 oz, 3-1/2" h	6.50	5	6.50
Tumbler, 10 oz, 4-3/4" h	8.50	9	7.50
Tumbler, 12 oz, 5" h	15	10	17.50

S-Pattern, crystal luncheon plate with yellow trim $9.50.

Additional Colors

Item	Fired-On Colors	Yellow
Berry bowl, 8-1/2" d	$-	$8.50
Cake plate, 11-3/4" d	-	50
Cake plate, 13" d	-	75
Cereal bowl, 5-1/2" d	12	6.50
Creamer, thick	15	7.50
Creamer, thin	15	7.50
Cup, thick	10	5
Cup, thin	10	5
Pitcher, 80 oz	-	
Plate, 6" d, sherbet	-	3.50
Plate, 8-1/4" d, luncheon	-	5
Plate, 9-1/4" d, dinner	-	9.50
Plate, grill	-	8.50
Saucer	-	4
Sherbet, low, ftd	-	8
Sugar, thick	15	7.50
Sugar, thin	15	7.50
Tumbler, 5 oz, 3-1/2" h	-	6.50
Tumbler, 10 oz, 4-3/4" h		8.50
Tumbler, 12 oz, 5" h		15

S-Pattern, yellow 5-1/2" cereal bowl $6.50, and 8-1/2" yellow berry bowl $8.50.

SANDWICH, DUNCAN & MILLER

LINE #41

Swatches

Amber

Cobalt Blue

Crystal

Green

Pink

Red

Manufactured by Duncan & Miller Glass Company, Washington, Pa., from 1924 to 1955.

Made in crystal with limited production in amber, cobalt blue, green, pink, and red. The molds were sold to Lancaster Colony which continues to produce some glass in this pattern, but in newer brighter colors, such as amberina, blue, and green.

Item	Crystal
Almond bowl, 2-1/2" d	**$12**
Ashtray, 2-1/2" x 3-3/4"	**10**
Ashtray, 2-3/4" sq	**8.50**
Basket, 6-1/2", loop handle	**135**
Basket 10", loop handle, crimped	**185**
Basket, 10", loop handle, oval	**185**
Basket, 11-1/2", loop handle	**225**
Bonbon, 5" w, heart shape	**15**

Item	Crystal
Bonbon, 6" w, heart shape, ring handle	20
Bonbon, cov, 7-1/2" d, ftd	45
Bowl, 5-1/2" d, handle	15
Butter, cov, quarter pound	40
Cake stand, 11-1/2" d, ftd	95
Cake stand, 12" d, ftd	115
Cake stand, 13" d, ftd	125
Candelabra, with bobeche and prisms, 10" h, three-lite	200
Candelabra, with bobeche and prisms, 10" h, one-lite	95
Candelabra, with bobeche and prisms, 16" h, three-lite	225
Candlesticks, pr, 4" h	30
Candlesticks, pr, 5" h, three-lite	90
Candy box, cov, 5" d, flat	42
Candy comport, 3-1/4" d, low, ftd or flared	25
Candy dish, 6" sq	375
Candy jar, cov, 8-1/2" d, flat	60
Celery tray, 10" l, oval	30
Champagne, 5 oz	25
Cheese comport, 13" d underplate	60
Cheese dish, cov	125
Cigarette box, cov, 3-1/2"	24
Cigarette holder, 3" ftd	30
Coaster, 5" d	12
Cocktail, 3 oz	15
Comport, 2-1/4"	17.50
Comport, 4-1/4" d, ftd	22
Comport, 5" d, low, ftd	22

Sandwich, 8" d crystal salad plate $10.

Item	Crystal
Comport, 5-1/2" d, ftd, low, crimped	25
Comport, 6" d, low, flared	25
Condiment set, pr cruets, pr salt and pepper shakers, tray	100
Console bowl, 12" d	45
Cracker plate, 13" d	32
Creamer	10
Cup	10
Deviled egg plate, 12" d	65
Epergne, 9" h	125
Epergne, 12" h, three parts	200
Finger bowl, 4" h	12
Finger bowl underplate, 6-1/2" d	8
Flower bowl, 11-1/2" d, crimped	60
Fruit bowl, 5" d	10
Fruit bowl, 10" d	65
Fruit bowl, 11-1/2" d, crimped, ftd	65
Fruit bowl, 12", flared	50
Fruit cup, 6 oz	12
Fruit salad bowl, 6" d	12
Gardenia bowl, 11-1/2" d	48
Goblet, 9 oz, 6" h	18
Grapefruit bowl, 5-1/2" d or 6" d	17.50
Hostess plate, 16" d	100
Ice cream dish 5 oz	12
Ice cream plate, rolled edge, 12" d	60
Ice cream tray, rolled edge, 12" d	45
Iced tea tumbler, 12 or 13 oz, ftd	20
Ivy bowl, ftd, crimped	35
Jelly, 3" d	8

Item	Crystal
Juice tumbler, 5 oz	12
Lazy Susan, 16" d	115
Lily bowl, 10" d	55
Mayonnaise set, three pcs	35
Mint tray, 6" l or 7" l, rolled edge, ring handle	18
Nappy, 5" d, two parts	15
Nappy, 5" d, ring handle	12
Nappy, 6" d, ring handle	15
Nut bowl, 3-1/2" d	10
Nut bowl, 11" d, cupped	55
Oil bottle, orig stopper	35
Oil and vinegar tray, 8" l	20
Oyster cocktail, 5 oz	18
Parfait, 4 oz, ftd	30
Pickle tray, 7" l, oval	15
Pitcher, 13 oz, metal lip	75
Pitcher, 64 oz, ice lip	125
Plate, 3" d, jelly	5
Plate, 6" d, bread and butter	6
Plate, 7" d, dessert	7.50
Plate, 8" d, salad	10
Plate, 9-1/2" d, dinner	35
Relish, 5-1/2" d, two parts, ring handle	15
Relish, 6" d, two parts, ring handle	18
Relish, 7" d, two parts, oval	20
Relish, 10" d, three parts, rect	27.50
Relish, 10" d, four parts	25
Relish, 10-1/2" l, three parts, rect	27.50
Relish, 12" l, three parts	25

Item	Crystal
Salad bowl, 10" d, deep	75
Salad bowl, 12" d, shallow	42
Salt and pepper shakers, pr, 2-1/2" h, glass tops	20
Salt and pepper shakers, pr, 2-1/2" h, metal tops	20
Salts and pepper shakers, set, pr 3-3/4" h, metal tops, 6" tray	35
Service plate, 11-1/2" d, handle	50
Service plate, 13" d	55
Sugar shaker	72
Sugar bowl, 5 oz	10
Sugar bowl, 9 oz, 3-1/4" h, ftd	12
Sundae, 5 oz	15
Torte plate, 12" d	48
Tray, 8" l	20
Urn, cov, 12" h, ftd	150
Tumbler, 9 oz, 4-3/4", ftd	15
Vase, 3" h, crimped	18
Vase, 3" h, flared rim	18
Vase, 4" h, hat shape	20
Vase, 4-1/2" h, crimped	25
Vase, 5" h, fan	40
Vase, 5" h, flared or crimped	25
Vase, 10" h, ftd	70
Wine, 3 oz	24

SANDWICH, HOCKING

HOCKING

Swatches

Crystal

Desert Gold

Forest Green

Pink

Royal Ruby

White

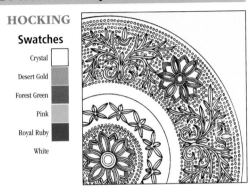

Manufactured by Hocking Glass Company, and later Anchor Hocking Corporation, from 1939 to 1964.

Made in crystal, Desert Gold, 1961-64; Forest Green, 1956-1960s; pink, 1939-1940; Royal Ruby, 1938-1939; and white/ivory (opaque), 1957-1960s.

Reproductions: † The cookie jar has been reproduced in crystal.

*No cover is known for the cookie jar in Forest Green.

Item	Crystal	Desert Gold	Forest Green
Bowl, 4-5/16" d, smooth	$5	$-	$4
Bowl, 4-7/8" d, smooth	5	6	-
Bowl, 4-7/8" d, crimped	20	-	-
Bowl, 5-1/4" d, scalloped	8	6	-
Bowl, 6-1/2" d, scalloped	7.50	9	60

Item	Crystal	Desert Gold	Forest Green
Bowl, 6-1/2" d, smooth	7.50	9	-
Bowl, 7-1/4" d, scalloped	14	-	-
Bowl, 8-1/4" d, oval	10	-	-
Bowl, 8-1/4" d, scalloped	18	-	80
Butter dish, cov	45	-	-
Cereal bowl, 6-3/4" d	32	12	-
Cookie jar, cov † *	40	45	20
Creamer	7.50	-	30
Cup, coffee	3.50	12	24
Cup, tea	5	15	24
Custard cup	7	-	4
Custard cup liner	5.50	-	1.50
Custard cup, crimped	15	-	-
Dessert bowl, 5" d, crimped	18.50	-	-
Juice pitcher, 6" h	115	-	145
Juice tumbler, 3 oz, 3-3/8" h	12	-	6
Juice tumbler, 5 oz, 3-9/16" h	6.50	-	4.50
Pitcher, half gallon, ice lip	85	-	550
Plate, 6" d	5	-	-
Plate, 7" d, dessert	20	-	-
Plate, 8" d, luncheon	18	-	-
Plate, 9" d, dinner	24	9	125
Plate, 9" d, indent for punch cup	12	-	-
Punch bowl, 9-3/4" d	18	-	-
Punch bowl and stand	30	-	-
Punch bowl set, bowl, base, 12 cups	80	-	-
Punch cup	4	-	-
Salad bowl, 7" d	8	25	-
Salad bowl, 7-5/8" d	-	-	60

Item	Crystal	Desert Gold	Forest Green
Salad bowl, 9" d	24	20	-
Sandwich plate, 12" d	14	17.50	-
Saucer	3.75	5	15
Sherbet, ftd	9	8	-
Snack set, plate and cup	12.50	-	-
Sugar, cov	30	-	-
Sugar, no cover	6	-	30
Tumbler, 9 oz, ftd	32.50	125	-
Tumbler, 9 oz, water	8	-	7
Vase	-	-	27.50
Vegetable, 8-1/2" l, oval	10	-	-

Sandwich, crystal oval bowl $10.

Additional Colors

Item	Pink	Royal Ruby	White
Bowl, 4-5/16" d, smooth	$-	$-	$-
Bowl, 4-7/8" d, smooth	7	17.50	-
Bowl, 4-7/8" d, crimped	-	-	-
Bowl, 5-1/4" d, scalloped	-	32	-
Bowl, 5-1/4" d, smooth	7	35	-
Bowl, 6-1/2" d, scalloped	-	35	-
Bowl, 8-1/4" d, scalloped	20	35	-
Plate, 9" d, dinner	10	-	-
Punch bowl, 9-3/4" d	-	-	15
Punch bowl and stand	-	-	30
Punch cup	-	-	2

Sandwich, 6-1/2" d smooth Desert Gold bowl, $9.

SANDWICH, INDIANA

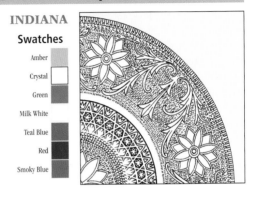

INDIANA

Swatches

Amber

Crystal

Green

Milk White

Teal Blue

Red

Smoky Blue

Manufactured by Indiana Glass Company, Dunkirk, Ind., 1920s to 1980s.

Made in crystal, late 1920s to 1990s; amber, late 1920s to 1980s; milk white, mid-1950s; teal blue, 1950s to 1960s; red, 1933 and early 1970s; smoky blue, 1976 to 1977; and green in the late 1960s and 1970s by Taira.

Reproductions: † Reproductions include a butter dish, decanter, and wine. Reproductions are found in dark amber, crystal, green, and pink.

Item	Amber	Crystal	Teal Blue	Red
Ashtray, club	$3.25	$3	$-	$-
Ashtray, diamond	3.25	3	-	-
Ashtray, heart	3.25	3	2	-

Item	Amber	Crystal	Teal Blue	Red
Ashtray, spade	3	3	-	-
Basket, 10" h	35	35	-	-
Berry bowl, 4-1/4" d	4	4	-	-
Bowl, 6" w, hexagonal	5.50	6	15	-
Bowl, 8-1/2" d	10	11	-	-
Butter dish, cov †	25	25	150	-
Candlesticks, pr, 3-1/2" h	18	20	-	-
Candlesticks, pr, 7" h	25	25	-	-
Celery tray, 10-1/2" l	16	14	-	-
Cereal bowl, 6" d	12	6.50	-	-
Cocktail, 3 oz, ftd	7.50	7.50	-	-
Comport, low, ruffled	15	-	-	-
Console bowl, 9" d	17.50	17.50	-	-
Console bowl, 11-1/2" d	20	20	-	-

Sandwich, crystal creamer and sugar with matching tray $18.

Item	Amber	Crystal	Teal Blue	Red
Creamer	6	6	-	48
Creamer and sugar, tray	18	18	35	-
Cruet, 6-1/2 oz, stopper	-	-	145	-
Cup	4	4	8.50	30
Decanter, stopper †	25	25	-	90
Fairy lamp	15	-	-	-
Goblet, 9 oz	12	12.50	-	45
Iced tea tumbler, 12 oz, ftd	10	10	-	-
Mayonnaise, ftd	14	14	-	-
Pitcher, 68 oz	24	24	-	175
Plate, 6" d, sherbet	3.50	3.50	7.50	-
Plate, 7" d, bread and butter	4	4	-	-
Plate, 8" d, oval, indent	5	4	6.50	15
Plate, 8-3/8" d, luncheon	7.50	8	-	20
Plate, 10-1/2" d, dinner	9	8.50	20	-
Puff box	18	18	-	-
Salt and pepper shakers, pr	18	18	-	-
Sandwich plate, 13" d	14.50	14.50	25	35
Sandwich server, center handle	20	20	-	50
Saucer	3.50	2.50	7	7.50
Sherbet, 3-1/4" h	6.50	5	12	-
Sugar, cov, large	20	15	-	48
Tumbler, 8 oz, ftd, water	10	10	-	-
Wine, 3" h, 4 oz †	10	12	-	15

SHARON

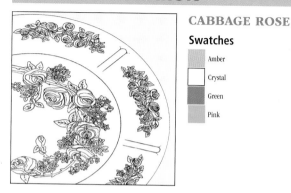

CABBAGE ROSE

Swatches

Amber

Crystal

Green

Pink

Manufactured by Federal Glass Company, Columbus, Ohio, from 1935 to 1939.

Made in amber, crystal, green, and pink.

Reproductions: † Reproductions include the butter dish, covered candy dish, creamer, covered sugar, and salt and pepper shakers. Reproduction colors include dark amber, blue, green, and pink.

Item	Amber	Crystal	Green	Pink
Berry bowl, 5" d	$8.50	$5	$18.50	$16.50
Berry bowl, 8-1/2" d	7.50	12	40	35
Butter dish, cov †	50	20	85	65
Cake plate, 11-1/2" d, ftd	30	10	65	45
Candy dish, cov †	45	15	100	65
Cereal, 6" d	24	12	32	30
Champagne, 5" d bowl	-	-	-	12
Cheese dish, cov †	225	1,500	-	950

Item	Amber	Crystal	Green	Pink
Cream soup, 5" d	28	15	60	52.50
Creamer, ftd †	15	14	22	24
Cup	9	6	18	18
Fruit bowl, 10-1/2" d	24	18	40	50
Iced tea tumbler, ftd	85	15	-	65
Jam dish, 7-1/2" d	45	-	48	215
Pitcher, 80 oz, ice lip	165	-	150	165
Pitcher, 80 oz, without ice lip	140	-	150	150
Plate, 6" d, bread and butter	12	5	9	9.50
Plate, 7-1/2" d, salad	22.50	6.50	8	30
Plate, 9-1/2" d, dinner	17	9.50	27.50	26.50
Platter, 12-1/2" l, oval	24	-	35	35
Salt and pepper shakers, pr †	50	-	80	65
Saucer	6.50	4	36	12
Sherbet, ftd	12.50	8	35	20
Soup, flat, 7-3/4" d, 1 7/8" deep	55	-	-	60
Sugar, cov †	35	12	55	60
Tumbler, 9 oz, 4-1/8" h, thick	30	-	65	47.50
Tumbler, 9 oz, 4-1/8" h, thin	38	-	65	50
Tumbler, 12 oz, 5-1/4" h, thick	55	-	95	50
Tumbler, 12 oz, 5-1/4" h, thin	55	-	95	62
Tumbler, 15 oz, 6-1/2" h, thick	125	18	-	65
Vegetable bowl, 9-1/2" l, oval	22	-	45	36

*Sharon, (counterclockwise) pink sherbet **$20**, 5" d berry bowl **$16.50**, creamer **$24,** and 8-1/2" d berry bowl **$35**.*

SHIPS

SAILBOAT, SPORTSMAN SERIES

Swatches

Cobalt Blue With Different Colors Of Decoration

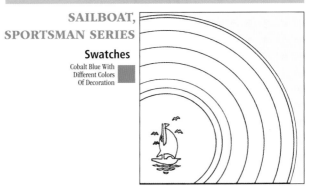

Manufactured by Hazel Atlas Glass Company, Clarksburg, W.V., and Zanesville, Ohio, late 1930s.

Made in cobalt blue with white, yellow, and red decoration. Pieces with yellow or red decoration are valued slightly higher than the traditional white decoration.

Item	Cobalt Blue with White Decoration
Ashtray	$60
Ashtray, metal sailboat	120
Box, cov, three parts	250
Cocktail mixer, stirrer	45
Cocktail shaker	25
Cup	15
Ice bowl	45
Iced tea tumbler, 10-1/2 oz, 4-7/8" h	22

Item	Cobalt Blue with White Decoration
Iced tea tumbler, 12 oz	24
Old fashioned tumbler, 8 oz, 3-3/8" h	22
Pitcher, 82 oz, no ice lip	85
Pitcher, 86 oz, ice lip	75
Plate, 5-7/8" d, bread & butter	40
Plate, 8" d, salad	27.50
Plate, 9" d, dinner	32
Saucer	18
Tumbler, 4 oz, 3-1/4" h, heavy bottom	27.50
Tumbler, 9 oz, 3-3/4" h	18
Whiskey, 3-1/2" h	45

Ships, cobalt blue salad plate $27.50.

*Ships, cobalt blue
cocktail shaker $45.*

SIERRA

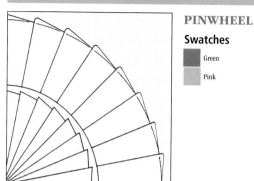

PINWHEEL

Swatches

Green

Pink

Manufactured by Jeannette Glass Company, Jeannette, Pa., from 1931 to 1933.

Made in green and pink. A few forms are known in Ultramarine.

Item	Green	Pink
Berry, small	$25	$25
Berry bowl, 8-1/2" d	40	47.50
Butter dish, cov	80	85
Cereal bowl, 5-1/2" d	35	30
Creamer	25	25
Cup	18.50	15
Pitcher, 32 oz, 6-1/2" h	170	150
Plate, 9" d, dinner	30	32
Platter, 11" l, oval	70	55
Salt and pepper shakers, pr	50	50
Saucer	12	8

Item	Green	Pink
Serving tray, 10-1/4" l, two handles	25	28
Sugar, cov	48	48
Tumbler, 9 oz, 4-1/2" h, ftd	90	80
Vegetable bowl, 9-1/4" l, oval	185	95

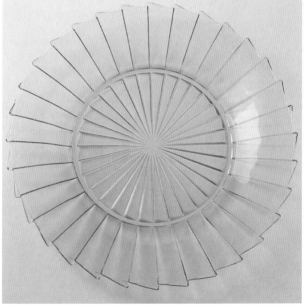

Sierra Pinwheel, pink dinner plate $32.

SPIRAL

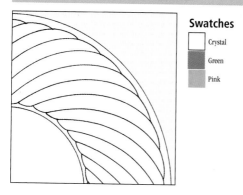

Manufactured by Hocking Glass Company, Lancaster, Ohio, from 1928 to 1930.

Made in crystal, green, and pink. Collector interest is strongest in green.

Item	Green
Berry bowl, 4-3/4" d	$8
Berry bowl, 8" d	16.50
Butter tub	27.50
Creamer, flat	8
Creamer, footed	8
Cup	6.50
Ice tub	25
Juice tumbler, 5 oz, 3" h	5
Mixing bowl, 7" d	9
Pitcher, 58 oz, 7-5/8" h	35

Item	Green
Plate, 6" d, sherbet	5
Plate, 8" d, luncheon	6.50
Platter, 12" l	32
Preserve, cov	50
Salt and pepper shakers, pr	37.50
Sandwich server, center handle	30
Saucer	5
Sherbet	5
Sugar, flat	8
Sugar, footed	8
Tumbler, 5-7/8" h, ftd	24
Tumbler, 9 oz, 5" h	12

Spiral, green luncheon plate $6.50, and sherbet $5.

STAR

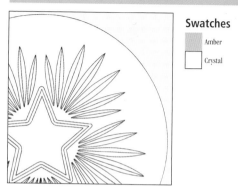

Swatches

▨ Amber

☐ Crystal

Manufactured by Federal Glass Company, Columbus, Ohio, 1950s.

Made in amber, crystal and crystal with gold trim. Crystal pieces with gold trim are valued the same as plain crystal.

Item	Amber	Crystal
Bowl, 5-5/8" d	$-	$7
Creamer	7	9
Cup	10	10
Dessert bowl, 4-5/8" d	4	5
Iced tea tumbler, 12 oz, 5-1/8" h	8	9
Juice pitcher, 36 oz, 5-3/4" h	10	18
Juice tumbler, 4-1/2 oz, 3-3/8" h	4	5
Pitcher, 60 oz, 7" h	15	14
Pitcher, 85 oz, 9-1/4" h, ice lip	15	15
Plate, 6-3/16" d, salad	5	6
Plate, 9-3/8" d, dinner	12	14

Item	Amber	Crystal
Saucer	4	3
Sugar, cov	15	15
Tumbler, 9 oz, 3-7/8" h, water	15	7.50
Vegetable bowl, 8-3/8" d	10	15
Whiskey, 1-1/2 oz, 2-1/4" h	4	5

Star, crystal bowl $7, 85 oz pitcher with ice lip $15, and 60 oz pitcher $14.

STARLIGHT

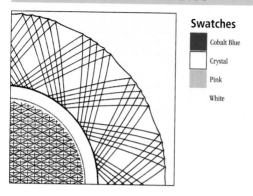

Swatches

■ Cobalt Blue

□ Crystal

▨ Pink

White

Manufactured by Hazel Atlas Glass Company, Clarksburg, W.V., and Zanesville, Ohio, from 1938 to 1940.

Made in cobalt blue, crystal, pink, and white. Production in cobalt blue was limited to an 8-1/2" d bowl, valued at $30.

Item	Crystal	Pink	White
Berry bowl, 4" d	$9.50	$-	$-
Bowl, 8-1/2" d, two handles	18	20	18
Bowl, 11-1/2" d, deep	25	-	25
Bowl, 12" d, 2-3/4" deep	25	-	25
Cereal bowl, 5-1/2" d, two handles	9.50	12	7
Creamer, oval	10	-	5
Cup	7	-	4
Plate, 6" d, sherbet	4.50	-	4
Plate, 7-1/2" d, salad	5	-	4.50
Plate, 8-1/2" d, luncheon	5	-	5

Item	Crystal	Pink	White
Plate, 9" d, dinner	8.50	-	8.50
Relish dish	15	-	15
Salad bowl, 11-1/2" d, deep	27.50	-	27.50
Salt and pepper shakers, pr	30	-	30
Sandwich plate, 13" d	25	20	-
Saucer	4	-	2.50
Sherbet	15	-	12
Sugar, oval	10	-	10

Starlight, 11-1/2" crystal bowl, $25, and 4-1/2"
crystal two-handled berry bowl, $9.50.

Starlight, crystal salt and pepper shakers $30.

STRAWBERRY

Swatches

Crystal
Green
Iridescent
Pink

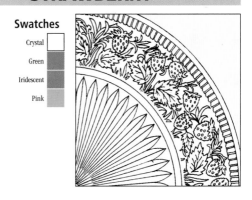

Manufactured by U.S. Glass Company, Pittsburgh, Pa., in the early 1930s.

Made in crystal, green, pink, and some iridescent.

Item	Crystal	Green	Iridescent	Pink
Berry bowl, 4" d	$7.50	$12	$7.50	$32.50
Berry bowl, 7-1/2" d	20	45	20	24
Bowl, 6-1/4" d, 2" deep	40	60	40	60
Butter dish, cov	125	225	135	195
Comport, 5-3/4" d	55	60	55	60
Creamer, large, 4-5/8" h	24	35	24	35
Creamer, small	12	18.50	12	18.50
Olive dish, 5" l, one handle	8.50	14	8.50	25
Pickle dish, 8-1/4" l, oval	8	14	8	15
Pitcher, 7-3/4" h	150	275	150	195
Plate, 6" d, sherbet	5	13.50	5	8

Strawberry, pink salad plate $15.

Item	Crystal	Green	Iridescent	Pink
Plate, 7-1/2" d, salad	10	14	10	15
Salad bowl, 6-1/2" d	15	20	15	20
Sherbet	6	13.50	6	13.50
Sugar, large, cov	60	85	60	85
Sugar, small, open	12	32	12	32
Tumbler, 8 oz, 3-5/8" h	20	32	20	40

Strawberry, pink covered sugar $85, and creamer $35.

SUNBURST

Manufactured by Jeannette Glass Company, Jeannette, Pa., late 1930s. Made in crystal.

Item	Crystal
Berry bowl, 4-3/4" d	$9
Berry bowl, 8-1/2" d	18
Bowl, 10-1/2" d	25
Candlesticks, pr, double	35
Creamer, ftd	16
Cup	7.50
Cup and saucer	10
Plate, 5-1/2" d	12
Plate, 9-1/4" d, dinner	25
Relish, two parts	14.50
Sandwich plate, 11-3/4" d	15
Saucer	4

Item	Crystal
Sherbet	12
Sugar	16
Tumbler, 4" h, 9 oz, flat	18.50

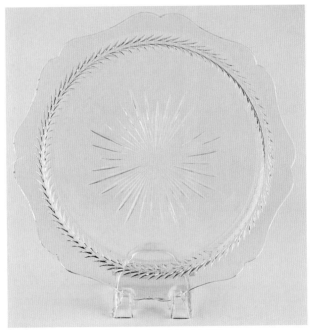

Sunburst, crystal sandwich plate $15.

SUNFLOWER

Swatches

Delphite

Green

Pink

Manufactured by Jeannette Glass Company, Jeannette, Pa., 1930s. Made in Delphite, green, pink, and some opaque colors.

Item	Delphite	Green	Pink	Opaque
Ashtray, 5" d	$-	$15	$15	$-
Cake plate, 10" d, three legs	-	20	20	-
Creamer	90	20	20	85
Cup	-	15	18	75
Plate, 9" d, dinner	-	27.50	24	-
Saucer	-	13.50	12	85
Sugar	-	25	22	-
Trivet, 7" d, three legs, turned up edge	-	325	315	-
Tumbler, 8 oz, 4-3/8" h, ftd	-	35	32	-

Sunflower, green cake plate $20.

SWIRL

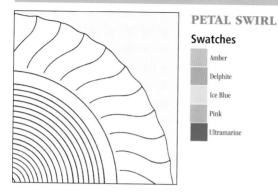

PETAL SWIRL

Swatches

	Amber
	Delphite
	Ice Blue
	Pink
	Ultramarine

Manufactured by Jeannette Glass Company, Jeannette, Pa., from 1937 to 1938.

Made in amber, Delphite, ice blue, pink, and Ultramarine. Production was limited in amber and ice blue.

Item	Delphite	Pink	Ultramarine
Berry bowl	$15	$-	$18.50
Bowl, 10" d, ftd, closed handles	-	25	35
Butter dish, cov	-	220	245
Candleholders, pr, double branch	-	40	60
Candleholders, pr, single branch	115	-	-
Candy dish, cov	-	235	150
Candy dish, open, three legs	-	20	20
Cereal bowl, 5-1/4" d	15	15	16
Coaster, 1" x 3-1/4"	-	18	18
Console bowl, 10-1/2" d, ftd	-	20	35

Item	Delphite	Pink	Ultramarine
Creamer	12	9.50	18
Cup and saucer	17.50	16	20
Plate, 6-1/2" d, sherbet	6.50	8	9
Plate, 7-1/4" d, luncheon	-	6.50	15
Plate, 8" d, salad	9	8.50	18
Plate, 9-1/4" d, dinner	12	17.50	25
Plate, 10-1/2" d, dinner	18	-	30
Platter, 12" l, oval	35	-	-
Salad bowl, 9" d	30	18	32.50
Salad bowl, 9" d, rimmed	-	20	30
Salt and pepper shakers, pr	-	-	55
Sandwich plate, 12-1/2" d	-	20	32.50
Sherbet, low, ftd	-	24	28
Soup, tab handles, lug	-	25	52.50
Sugar, ftd	-	12	18
Tray, 10-1/2" l, two handles	25	-	-
Tumbler, 9 oz, 4" h	-	18	35
Tumbler, 9 oz, 4-5/8" h	-	18	-
Tumbler, 13 oz, 5-1/8" h	-	45	90
Vase, 6-1/2" h, ftd, ruffled	-	22	-
Vase, 8-1/2" h, ftd	-	-	30

Swirl, Ultramarine 10-1/2" dinner plate $30, and closed-handled bowl $35.

TEA ROOM

Swatches

Amber

Crystal

Green

Pink

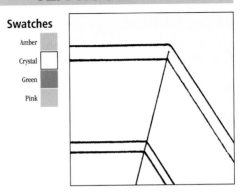

Manufactured by Indiana Glass Company, Dunkirk, Ind., from 1926 to 1931.

Made in amber, crystal, green, and pink.

Item	Amber	Crystal	Green	Pink
Banana split bowl, 7-1/2" l	$-	$95	$200	$215
Candlesticks, pr, low	-	-	80	95
Celery Bowl, 8-1/2"d	-	15	35	27.50
Creamer, 3-1/4" h	-	-	30	28
Creamer, 4-1/2" h, ftd	80	-	20	25
Creamer and sugar on tray	-	-	95	85
Cup	-	-	65	60
Finger bowl	-	80	50	40
Goblet, 9 oz.	-	-	75	65
Ice bucket	-	-	85	80
Lamp, electric	-	140	175	195

Item	Amber	Crystal	Green	Pink
Mustard, cov	-	145	160	140
Parfait	-	-	72	65
Pitcher, 64 oz	425	400	150	200
Plate, 6-1/2" d, sherbet	-	-	35	32
Plate, 8-1/4" d, luncheon	-	-	37.50	35
Plate, 10-1/2" d, two handles	-	-	50	45
Relish, divided	-	-	30	25
Salad bowl, 8-3/4" d, deep	-	-	150	135
Salt and pepper shakers, pr, ftd	-	-	60	55

Tea Room, footed pink sugar $30, and creamer $25.

Item	Amber	Crystal	Green	Pink
Saucer	-	-	30	25
Sherbet	-	22	40	35
Sugar, 3" h, cov	-	-	115	100
Sugar, 4-1/2" h, ftd	80	-	30	30
Sugar, cov, flat	-	-	200	170
Sundae, ftd, ruffled	-	-	85	70
Tumbler, 6 oz, ftd	-	-	55	32
Tumbler, 8 oz, 5-1/4" h, ftd	75	-	32	40
Tumbler, 11 oz., ftd	-	-	45	45
Tumbler, 12 oz, ftd	-	-	60	55
Vase, 6-1/2" h, ruffled edge	-	-	145	90
Vase, 9-1/2" h, ruffled	-	45	175	100
Vase, 9-1/2"h, straight	-	130	95	225
Vase, 11" h, ruffled edge	-	-	350	395
Vase, 11" h, straight	-	-	200	395
Vegetable bowl, 9-1/2" l, oval	-	-	75	65

THISTLE

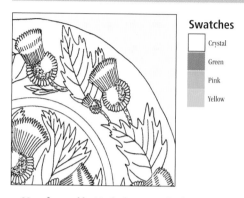

Swatches

☐ Crystal

☐ Green

☐ Pink

☐ Yellow

Manufactured by Macbeth-Evans, Charleroi, Pa., about 1929 to 1930.
Made in crystal, green, pink, and yellow. Production was limited in
crystal and yellow.

Reproductions: † Recent reproductions have been found in pink, a
darker emerald green, and wisteria. Several of the reproductions have a
scalloped edge. Reproductions include the cake plate, fruit bowl, pitcher,
salt and pepper shakers, and a small tumbler.

Item	Green	Pink
Cake plate, 13" d, heavy †	$195	$225
Cereal bowl, 5-1/2" d	50	50
Cup, thin	36.50	24
Fruit bowl, 10-1/4" d †	295	495
Plate, 8" d, luncheon	30	32
Plate, 10-1/4" d, grill	35	30
Saucer	12	12

Thistle, green luncheon plate $30.

THUMBPRINT

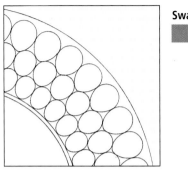

Swatches

Green

Manufactured by Federal Glass Company, Columbus, Ohio, from 1927 to 1930.

Made in green.

Item	Green
Berry bowl, 4-3/4" d	**$10**
Berry bowl, 8" d	**25**
Cereal bowl, 5" d	**10**
Creamer, ftd	**12**
Cup	**8**
Fruit bowl, 5" d	**10**
Juice tumbler, 4" h	**6**
Plate, 6" d, sherbet	**4.50**
Plate, 8" d, luncheon	**7**
Plate, 9-1/4" d, dinner	**24**
Salt and pepper shakers, pr	**65**
Saucer	**4**

Item	Green
Sherbet	9
Sugar, ftd	12
Tumbler, 5" h	25
Tumbler, 5-1/2" h	10
Whiskey, 2-1/4" h	6.50

Thumbprint, green luncheon plate $7.

TULIP

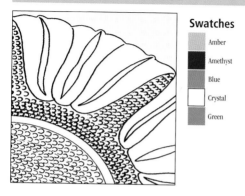

Swatches

- Amber
- Amethyst
- Blue
- Crystal
- Green

Manufactured by Dell Glass Company, Millville, N.J., early 1930s.
Made in amber, amethyst, blue, crystal, and green.

Item	Amber	Ameth.	Blue	Crystal	Green
Bowl, 6" d	$20	$18	$18	$20	$20
Bowl, 13-1/4" l, oblong oval	90	100	110	90	90
Candleholders, pr, 3-3/4" h	24.50	30	30	24.50	24.50
Candy, cov	175	195	195	150	165
Creamer	20	25	30	20	30
Cup	15	20	24	15	18
Decanter, orig stopper	-	500	500	-	-
Ice tub, 4-7/8" wide, 3" deep	70	95	95	65	90
Juice tumbler	15	40	40	15	15

Item	Amber	Ameth.	Blue	Crystal	Green
Plate, 7-1/4" d	12	20	22	13.50	24
Plate, 10-1/4" d	35	40	42.50	20	40
Saucer	10	8.50	10	5	7.50
Sherbet, 3-3/4" h, flat	20	24	24	18	20
Sugar	20	25	25	20	20
Whiskey	22	35	35	20	25

Tulip, green creamer $30.

TWIGGY

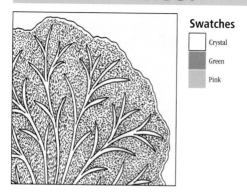

Swatches

☐	Crystal
▨	Green
▨	Pink

Manufactured by Indiana Glass Company, Dunkirk, Ind., in the 1950s and early 1960s.

Made in crystal, some green and pink, and rarely in light blue with an opalescent edge. Collector interest is highest in the crystal.

Item	Crystal
Jelly, 8" d	**$12**
Nappy, 4-1/2" d	5
Nappy, 8" d	8
Plate, 8" d	10
Punch bowl	45
Punch cup	12
Relish, 10" d, divided	15
Relish, 8" d	12
Snack plate, 10" d	10

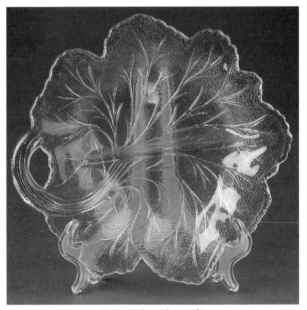

Twiggy, 8" d crystal nappy $8.

Twiggy, 10" d crystal divided relish $15.

TWISTED OPTIC

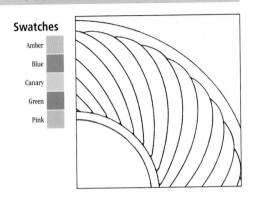

Swatches

Amber

Blue

Canary

Green

Pink

Manufactured by Imperial Glass Company, Bellaire, Ohio, from 1927 to 1930.

Made in amber, blue, canary, green, and pink.

Item	Amber	Blue	Canary	Green	Pink
Basket, 10" h	$55	$95	$95	$60	$60
Bowl, 7" d, ruffled	-	-	-	-	18
Bowl, 9" d	18.50	28.50	28.50	18.50	18.50
Bowl, 11-1/2" d, 4-1/4" h	24	48	48	24	24
Candlesticks, pr, 3" h	22	40	40	35	22
Candlesticks, pr, 8" h	30	50	50	30	30
Candy jar, cov, flat	25	50	50	25	25
Candy jar, cov, flat, flange edge	50	90	90	55	55
Candy jar, cov, ftd, flange edge	50	90	90	55	55
Candy jar, cov, ftd, short	55	100	100	60	60

Item	Amber	Blue	Canary	Green	Pink
Candy jar, cov, ftd, tall	55	100	100	60	60
Cereal bowl, 5"d	8.50	15	15	10	10
Cologne bottle, stopper	60	85	85	60	60
Console bowl, 10-1/2" d	25	45	45	25	25
Cream soup, 4-3/4" d	12	25	25	15	15
Creamer	8	14	14	8	8
Cup	7.50	12.50	12.50	5	8
Mayonnaise	20	50	50	30	30
Pitcher, 64 oz	45	-	-	40	45
Plate, 6" d, sherbet	3	6.50	6.50	3	3
Plate, 7" d, salad	4	8	8	4	4
Plate, 7-1/2" x 9" l, oval	6	12	12	6	6
Plate, 8" d, luncheon	6	9	10	6	5
Powder jar, cov	38	65	65	38	38
Preserve jar	30	-	-	30	30
Salad bowl, 7" d	12	25	25	15	15
Sandwich plate, 10" d	12	20	20	15	15
Sandwich server, center handle	22	35	35	22	22
Sandwich server, two handles, flat	15	20	20	15	15
Saucer	2.50	4.50	4.50	2.50	5
Sherbet	7.50	12	12.50	7	7.50
Sugar	8	14	14	8	10
Tumbler, 4-1/2" h, 9 oz	6.50	-	-	6.50	7
Tumbler, 5-1/4" h, 12 oz	9.50	-	-	9.50	10
Vase, 7-1/4" h, two handles, rolled edge	35	65	65	40	40
Vase, 8" h, two handles, fan	45	95	95	50	50
Vase, 8" h, two handles, straight edge	45	95	95	50	50

U.S. SWIRL

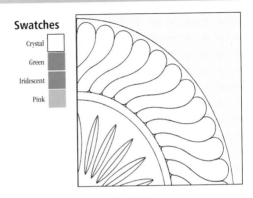

Swatches

Crystal
Green
Iridescent
Pink

Manufactured by U.S. Glass Company, late 1920s.

Made in crystal, green, iridescent, and pink. Production in crystal and iridescent was limited.

Item	Green	Pink
Berry bowl, 4-3/8" d	$8	$10
Berry bowl, 7-7/8" d	15	17
Bowl, 5-1/2" d, handle	10	12
Bowl, 8-1/4" l, 2 3/4" h, oval	40	40
Bowl, 8-3/8" l, 1-3/4" h, oval	50	50
Butter dish, cov	115	115
Candy, cov, two handles	30	32
Creamer	15	17.50
Pitcher, 48 oz, 8" h	55	50
Plate, 6-1/8" d, sherbet	3	2.50
Plate, 7-7/8" d, salad	6	6.50

Item	Green	Pink
Salt and pepper shakers, pr	48	45
Sherbet, 3-1/4" h	5	6
Sugar, cov	35	32
Tumbler, 8 oz, 3-5/8" h	12	12
Tumbler, 12 oz, 4-3/4" h	15	17.50
Vase, 6-1/2" h	25	25

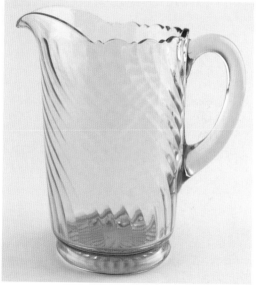

U.S. Swirl, green pitcher $55.

VERNON

Swatches

Crystal

Green

Yellow

Manufactured by Indiana Glass Company, Dunkirk, Ind., from 1930 to 1932.

Made in crystal, green, and yellow.

Item	Crystal	Green	Yellow
Creamer, ftd	$12	$25	$30
Cup	10	15	18
Plate, 8" d, luncheon	7	10	15
Sandwich plate, 11-1/2" d	14	25	30
Saucer	4	6	6
Sugar, ftd	18	25	30
Tumbler, 5" h, ftd	16	40	45

Vernon, yellow tumbler $45.

VICTORY

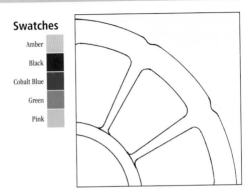

Swatches

Amber

Black

Cobalt Blue

Green

Pink

Manufactured by Diamond Glass-Ware Company, Indiana, Pa., from 1929 to 1932.

Made in amber, black, cobalt blue, green, and pink.

Item	Amber	Black	Cobalt Blue	Green	Pink
Bonbon, 7" d	$15	$20	$20	$15	$15
Bowl, 11" d, rolled edge	30	50	50	30	30
Bowl, 12-1/2" d, flat edge	30	60	60	30	30
Candlesticks, pr, 3" h	35	100	100	35	35
Cereal bowl, 6-1/2" d	15	30	30	15	15
Cheese and cracker set, 12" d indented plate and comport	45	-	-	45	45
Comport, 6" h, 6-1/4" d	18	-	-	18	18
Console bowl, 12" d	35	65	65	35	35

Item	Amber	Black	Cobalt Blue	Green	Pink
Creamer	17.50	45	45	15	15
Cup	10	35	40	10	10
Goblet, 7 oz, 5" h	20	-	-	20	20
Gravy boat, underplate	185	325	325	185	185
Mayonnaise set, 3-1/2" h, 5-1/2" d bowl, 8-1/2" d indented plate, ladle	55	100	100	55	55
Plate, 6" d, bread and butter	6.50	17.50	17.50	6.50	6.50
Plate, 7" d, salad	7.50	20	20	8	7
Plate, 8" d, luncheon	10	40	30	8	8
Plate, 9" d, dinner	20	40	40	22	20
Platter, 12" l, oval	30	70	70	32	32
Sandwich server, center handle	35	65	65	40	30
Saucer	5	12.50	12.50	5	6
Sherbet, ftd	15	27.50	27.50	15	15
Soup bowl, 8-1/2" d, flat	20	45	45	20	20
Sugar	15	45	45	15	15
Vegetable bowl, 9" l, oval	35	85	85	35	35

Victory, pink creamer $15, and sugar $15.

VITROCK

FLOWER RIM

Swatches

White

Manufactured by Hocking Glass Company, Lancaster, Ohio, from 1934 to 1937.

Made in white and white with fired-on colors.

Item	Fired-On Colors	White
Berry bowl, 4" d	$9.50	$7.50
Cereal bowl, 7-1/2" d	12	8.50
Cream soup, 5-1/2" d	16	14
Creamer, oval	10	7.50
Cup	8.50	6
Fruit bowl, 6" d	10	8
Plate, 7-1/4" d, salad	7.50	6
Plate, 8-3/4" d, luncheon	12	6.50
Plate, 10" d, dinner	15	12
Platter, 11-1/2" l	50	35

Item	Fired-On Colors	White
Saucer	7.50	3.50
Soup bowl, flat	48	35
Sugar	12	8.50
Vegetable bowl, 9-1/2" d	24	18

Vitrock, white salad plate $6, and cereal bowl $8.50.

WATERFORD

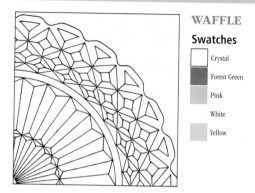

WAFFLE

Swatches

- ☐ Crystal
- ■ Forest Green
- ☐ Pink
- ☐ White
- ☐ Yellow

Manufactured by Hocking Glass Company, Lancaster, Ohio, from 1938 to 1944.

Made in crystal, Forest Green (1950s), pink, white, and yellow. Forest Green and yellow production was limited. Collector interest is low in white.

Item	Crystal	Pink
Ashtray, 4" d	$8	$-
Berry bowl, 4-3/4" d	8.50	18
Berry bowl, 8-1/4" d	10	36
Bonbon, cov	45	-
Butter dish, cov	30	250
Cake plate, 10-1/4" d, handles	15	25
Cereal bowl, 5-1/2" d	18.50	32
Coaster, 4" d	5.50	-
Creamer, Miss America style	35	-

Item	Crystal	Pink
Creamer, oval	5	15
Cup	8.50	18
Cup, Miss America style	-	45
Goblet, 5-1/2" h, Miss America style	35	85
Goblet, 5-1/4" h	16	-
Goblet, 5-5/8" h	20	-
Juice pitcher, 42 oz, tilted	30	-
Juice tumbler, 5 oz, 3-1/2" h, Miss America style	-	65
Lamp, 4" spherical base	45	-
Pitcher, 80 oz, tilted, ice lip	50	165
Plate, 6" d, sherbet	5	9.50
Plate, 7-1/8" d, salad	8	18
Plate, 9-5/8" d, dinner	12.50	24
Platter, 14" l	14	-
Relish, 13-3/4" d, five parts	12	-
Salt and pepper shakers, pr	14.50	-
Sandwich plate, 13-3/4" d	15	32
Saucer	5	5
Sherbet, ftd	5	15
Sherbet, ftd, scalloped base	8	-
Sugar	6.50	15
Sugar, Miss America style	30	-
Sugar lid, oval	5	25
Tray, 10-1/4" l, handles	15	-
Tumbler, 10 oz, 4-7/8" h, ftd	12	30

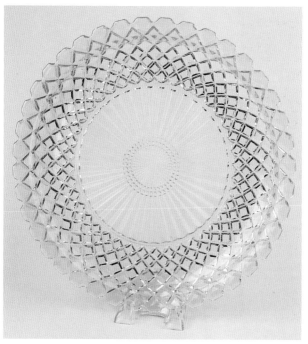

Waterford, crystal dinner plate $12.50.

WEXFORD

Swatches

Crystal

Manufactured by Anchor Hocking Glass Corp.

Made in crystal.

Item	Crystal
Bowl, 7-3/4" d, ftd	**$30**
Bud vase	**12**
Butter dish, cov	**30**
Candlestick	**9**
Candy dish, cov, 7-3/4" d	**15**
Canister, cov, coffee, 5-3/8" h	**15**
Canister, cov, flour, 9-1/4" h	**22**
Canister, cov, sugar, 6-3/8" h	**18**
Centerpiece bowl	**18**
Champagne, 3-5/8" h	**8**
Chip and dip set	**20**
Claret, 5-3/8" h	**10**

Item	Crystal
Creamer, 4-1/4" h	10
Cruet, 7-1/2" h	15
Cup, ftd, 3" h	6
Decanter, 11-3/4" h	30
Decanter, 14-1/2" h	35
Dessert bowl, 5-1/2" d	4
Fruit bowl, 10" d, ftd	30
Goblet, 6-5/8" h	12
Iced tea tumbler, 5-1/2" h, 12 oz	12
Juice tumbler	9
Old fashioned tumbler, 3-3/4" h	9
Pitcher, 5-1/4" h, pint	18
Pitcher, 9-3/4" h, two quart	35
Plate, luncheon	9
Plate, salad	6
Punch bowl	10
Punch cup, 3" d	3
Relish	20
Relish, three parts, 8-5/8" l	18
Salad bowl, 9-3/4" d	15
Serving plate	20
Sherbet, low	6.50
Sugar, cov, 5-1/4" h, ftd	15
Toothpick holder	12
Torte plate, 14" d	24
Tumbler, 5-1/2" h, flat	6
Vase, ftd	40
Wine, 4-1/2" h	10

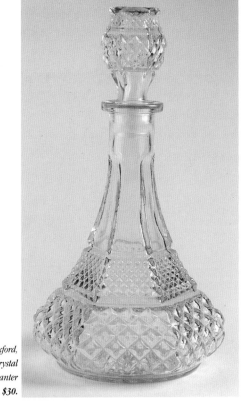

*Wexford,
11-3/4" h crystal
decanter
$30.*

Wexford, crystal serving plate $20.

WINDSOR

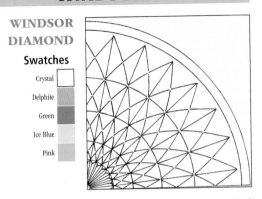

**WINDSOR
DIAMOND**

Swatches

Crystal

Delphite

Green

Ice Blue

Pink

Manufactured by Jeannette Glass Company, Jeannette, Pa., from 1936 to 1946.

Made in crystal, green, and pink, with limited production in amberina red, Delphite, and ice blue.

Item	Crystal	Green	Pink
Ashtray, 5-3/4" d	$15	$55	$45
Berry bowl, 4-3/4" d	5	5	12
Berry bowl, 8-1/2" d	7.50	18.50	25
Bowl, 5" l, pointed edge	10	-	70
Bowl, 7" x 11-3/4", boat shape	30	40	32
Bowl, 7-1/2" d, three legs	8	-	24
Bowl, 8" d, two handles	9	24	20
Bowl, 8" l, pointed edge	10	-	48
Bowl, 10-1/2" l, pointed edge	25	-	32
Butter dish, cov	30	95	60

Item	Crystal	Green	Pink
Cake plate, 10-3/4" d, ftd	12	22	20
Candlesticks, pr, 3" h	24	-	265
Candy jar, cov	18	-	-
Cereal bowl, 5-3/8" d	10	32.50	32
Chop plate, 13-5/8" d	24	55	45
Coaster, 3-1/4" d	8.50	22	25
Comport	9	-	-
Cream soup, 5" d	6	30	25
Creamer	8	15	20
Creamer, holiday shape	7.50	-	-
Cup	7	18	12
Fruit console, 12-1/2" d	45	-	115
Pitcher, 16 oz, 4-1/2" h	25	-	115
Pitcher, 52 oz, 6-3/4" h	20	65	40
Plate, 6" d, sherbet	3.75	8	6
Plate, 7" d, salad	4.50	30	18
Plate, 9" d, dinner	10	25	25
Platter, 11-1/2" l, oval	7	25	30
Powder jar	20	-	55
Relish platter, 11-1/2" l, divided	30	-	200
Salad bowl, 10-1/2" d	12	-	-
Salt and pepper shakers, pr	20	55	45
Sandwich plate, 10" d, closed handles	10	-	24
Sandwich plate, 10" d, open handles	12.50	18	20
Saucer	2.50	5	4.50
Sherbet, ftd	3.50	18	15
Sugar, cov	24	40	42
Sugar, cov, holiday shape	12	-	135
Tray, 4" sq	5	12	10
Tray, 4" sq, handles	6	-	40

Item	Crystal	Green	Pink
Tray, 4-1/8" x 9"	5	16	10
Tray, 4-1/8" x 9", handles	9	-	50
Tray, 8-1/2" x 9-3/4"	7	35	25
Tray, 8-1/2" x 9-3/4", handles	15	45	85
Tumbler, 4" h, ftd	7	-	-
Tumbler, 5 oz, 3-1/4" h	9	36.50	26.50
Tumbler, 7-1/4" h, ftd	19	-	-
Tumbler, 9 oz, 4" h	7.50	36.50	18
Tumbler, 11 oz, 4-5/8" h	8	-	-
Tumbler, 12 oz, 5" h	11	55	32.50
Tumbler, 11 oz, 5" h, ftd	12	-	-
Vegetable bowl, 9-1/2" l, oval	7.50	32.50	25

Windsor, crystal chop plate $24, and 16 oz pink pitcher $115.

YORKTOWN

Swatches

Crystal

Iridescent

Smoke

White

Yellow

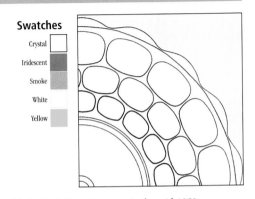

Manufactured by Federal Glass Company, in the mid-1950s.

Made in crystal, iridescent, smoke, white, and yellow. Values for all the colors are about the same.

Item	Crystal, etc.
Berry bowl, 5-1/2" d	$4.50
Berry bowl, 9-1/2" d	10
Celery tray, 10" l	10
Creamer	5
Cup	3.50
Fruit bowl, 10" d, ftd	18
Iced tea tumbler, 5-1/4" h, 13 oz	7.50
Juice tumbler, 3-7/8" h, 6 oz	4.50
Mug	15
Plate, 8-1/4" d	4.50
Plate, 11-1/2" d	8.50

Item	Crystal, etc.
Punch bowl set	40
Punch cup	2.50
Relish	5
Sandwich server	7.50
Saucer	1
Sherbet, 7 oz	3.50
Snack cup	2.50
Snack plate with indent	3.50
Sugar	5
Tumbler, 4-3/4" h, 10 oz	6
Vase, 8" h	15

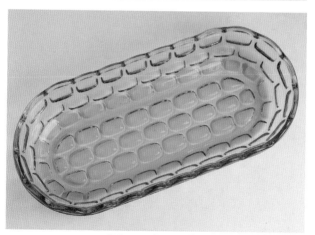

Yorktown, yellow relish $5.

Yorktown, yellow sandwich server with gold metal center handle $7.50.

GLOSSARY

AOP: All-over pattern, often found in descriptions to indicate a design that covers the entire piece rather than in just one location.

Berry bowl: Used to describe both individual serving dishes and master bowl used as a set to serve berries (strawberries, etc.). Often accompanied by creamer or milk pitcher and sugar bowl.

Bouillon: Generally, cup-shaped bowl for serving broth or clear soups; usually has handles.

Cheese and cracker set: Serving piece often consists of a comport to hold cheese and large plate for crackers; forms differ. Sometimes a sherbet is used as a comport.

Cheese dish: Serving dish, often with domed top, to cover cheese wedge.

Children's wares: Dish and tea sets designed to be used by children for play.

Chop plate: Large round plate used to serve individual portions of meat and fowl.

Cider set: Consists of covered cookie jar (used to hold cider), tray and roly-poly cups and ladle.

Closed handle: Solid glass handle.

Comport: Container used as serving dish, usually open, but some patterns include a covered form. Also known as a compote.

Compote: Another name for comport.

Console set: Decorative large bowl with matching candlesticks.

Cream soup: Bowl used to serve cream-type or chilled soups; usually has handles.

Cup and saucer: Used to refer to place-setting cup and saucer; some patterns include larger coffee cup or more diminutive tea cup.

Demitasse cup and saucer: Term used to describe smaller cup and saucer used for after-dinner beverage.

Domino tray: Tray used to hold sugar blocks shaped like dominoes.

Egg cup: Stemware with short stem used to hold an egg; usually used with underplate.

Goblet: Stemware used to hold water.

Grill plate: Dinner-sized plate with lines that divide plate into compartments.

Ice lip: Small piece of glass inside of top of pitcher to hold ice in pitcher. May also mean a pinched lip that prevents ice from falling from pitcher.

Icer: Vessel with compartment to hold crushed ice to keep main vessel cold, i.e., mayonnaise, cream soup, shrimp, etc.

Individual-sized pieces: Smaller sized pieces, often designed for bed tray use. Not to be confused with children's wares.

Liner: Underplate or under bowl used to accompany another piece, i.e., finger bowl or sherbet.

Light (Lite): Branch found on candlestick used to hold additional candles, i.e., 2 light, 3 light.

Nappy: Shallow bowl used as serving dish or in place-setting; often has small handle.

Oil/vinegar: Term used to describe cruet or bottle with stopper to hold oil and/or vinegar for salads.

Platter: Small, medium or large oval plate used to serve roasts and fowl.

Ring handle: Figural round handle, ring-shaped.

Salver: Large round plate used as serving piece.

Sandwich server: Round plate, often with center handle (made of glass or metal) used to serve tea-type sandwiches.

Sherbet: Part of a place-setting used to hold sherbet, often served with matching underplate about the same size as a saucer.

Snack set: Plate or small tray with indent to hold punch or coffee-type cup.

Spooner: Small, often squatty, open vase-type vessel used to hold spoons upright. Typically part of table set.

Spoon tray: Small bowl-shaped vessel used to hold spoons horizontally, often oval. Often used on buffets, etc., to hold extra place-setting spoons.

Stand: Base or additional piece used to hold punch bowl, etc.

Table set: Name given to set of matching covered butter dish, creamer, covered (or open) sugar and spooner. An extended table service may include syrup, toothpick holder, and salt and pepper shakers.

Tab handle: Small solid glass handle useful to grab bowl, etc.

Toddy set: Set consists of covered cookie jar (used to hold toddy), tray and roly-poly cups and ladle.

Tumbler: Any footed or flat vessel used to hold water or other liquids. Specialized tumblers include ginger ale, juice, iced tea, lemonade, old fashioned, and whiskey.

Wine: Term used to describe stemware used to hold wine. Depression-era wines have a small capacity by today's standards.

Hobnail, pink sherbet.

REFERENCES

GENERAL DEPRESSION GLASS REFERENCES

Brenner, Robert, *Depression Glass for Collectors*, Schiffer, 1998.

Coe, Debbie and Randy, *Elegant Glass: Early, Depression & Beyond*, Schiffer Publishing, 2007.

Florence, Gene and Cathy, *Collectible Glassware from the 40s, 50s, & 60s*, 9th Edition, Collector Books, 2007.

—*Collector's Encyclopedia of Depression Glass*, 18th Edition, Collector Books, 2007.

—*Elegant Glassware of the Depression Era*, 12th Edition, Collector Books, 2006.

—*Kitchen Glassware of the Depression Era*, 6th Edition, Collector Books, 2004.

—*Pocket Guide To Depression Glass & More*, 15th edition, Collector Books, 2006.

Kovel, Ralph and Terry, *Kovel's Depression Glass Dinnerware Price List*, 8th Edition, Random House, 2004.

Mauzy, Barbara and Jim, *Mauzy's Comprehensive Handbook of Depression Glass Prices*, 6th Edition, Schiffer Publishing, 2007.

—*Mauzy's Depression Glass, A Photographic Reference with Prices*, Schiffer Publishing, revised 2007.

Weatherman, Hazel Marie, *Colored Glassware of the Depression Era, Book 2*, published by author, 1974, available in reprint.

—*1984 Supplement & Price Trends for Colored Glassware of the Depression Era, Book 1*, published by author, 1984.

Yeske, Doris, *Depression Glass: A Collector's Guide*, rev. and expanded, 7th ed, Schiffer Publishing, 2005.

—*Depression Glass and Beyond: A Guide to Pattern Identification*, Schiffer Publishing, 2003.

—*Depression Glass Dinnerware Accessories*, Schiffer Publishing, 2005.

Sandwich pattern by Duncan & Miller

SPECIFIC COMPANY REFERENCES

Duncan:

Krause, Gail, *The Encyclopedia of Duncan Glass*, published by author, 1984.

—*A Pictorial History of Duncan & Miller Glass*, published by author, 1986.

—*The Years of Duncan*, published by author, 1980.

Piña, Leslie, *Depression Era Glass By Duncan*, Schiffer Publishing, 1992.

Fenton:

Moran, Mark, *Warman's Fenton Glass*, 2nd Ed., Krause Publications, 2007.

Fostoria:

Bones, Frances, *Fostoria Glassware 1887-1982*, Collector Books, 1999.

Kerr, Ann, *Fostoria: An Identification and Value Guide*, *Volume I, Pressed, Blown & Hand Molded Shapes*, Collector Books, 1994, 1997 values.

—*Fostoria: An Identification and Value Guide, Volume II, Etched and Carved & Cut Designs*, Collector Books, 1996.

Long, Milbra and Emily Seate, *Fostoria Stemware, The Crystal for America*, Collector Books, 1997.

—*Fostoria Tableware, 1924-1943*, Collector Books, 1999.

—*Fostoria Tableware, 1944-1986*, Collector Books, 1999.

—*The Fostoria Value Guide,* Schiffer, 2003.

Piña, Leslie, *Fostoria American Line 2056*, Schiffer Publishing, 1999.

—*Fostoria Designer George Sakier*, Schiffer Publishing, 1996.

—*Fostoria: Serving the American Table 1887-1986*, Schiffer Publishing, 2002.

Schliesmann, Jo Ann, *Price Guide to Fostoria,* 3rd Edition, Park Avenue Publications, 1987.

Imperial:

Archer, Margaret and Douglas, *Imperial Glass,* Collector Books, 1978, 1993 value updates.

Garrison, Myrna and Bob, *Imperial Cape Cod: Tradition to Treasure,* 2nd Edition, published by authors, 1991.

Marsh, Laura J., *Imperial Glass Co: Lace Edge,* Schiffer Publishing, 2004.

National Imperial Glass Collectors Society, Imperial Glass Encyclopedia, Volume I: A-Cane, Antique Publications, 1995.

—*Imperial Glass Encyclopedia, Volume II: Cape Cod to L,* Antique Publications, 1998.

—*Imperial Glass Encyclopedia, Volume III, M-Z,* Antique Publications, 1999.

National Imperial Glass Collectors Society, Imperial Glass 1966 Catalog, reprint, 1991 price guide, Antique Publications.

Indiana Glass:

Schenning, Craig, *A Century of Indiana Glass,* Schiffer Publishing, 2005.

Lancaster Glass:

Zastowney, John P. , *Lancaster Glass Co., 1908-1937,* Collector Books, 2007.

L.E. Smith:

Felt, Tom, *L.E. Smith Glass Company, The First One Hundred Years,* Collector Books, 2007.

Tiffin:

Bickenhauser, Fred, *Tiffin Glassmasters*, Book I (1979), Book II (1981), Book III (1985), Glassmasters Publications.

Goshe, Ed, *40s, 50s, & 60s Stemware by Tiffin*, Schiffer Publishing, 1999.

Goshe, Ed, Ruth Hemminger, and Leslie Piña, *Tiffin Depression-Era Stems and Tablewares*, Schiffer Publishing, 1998.

Westmoreland:

Kovar, Lorraine, *Westmoreland Glass, Volumes I and II* (1991), *Volume III* (1998), Antique Publications, 1991.

—*Westmoreland Glass 1950-1984 Volume I Comprehensive Price Guide*, published by author, 2007.

—*Price Guide to Westmoreland's Paneled Grape Pattern*, published by author, 1997.

Della Robbia pattern by Westmoreland

RESOURCES

COLLECTORS' CLUBS

International Associations

Anchor Hocking Glass Club
3950 Taravue
St. Louis County, MO 63125

Canadian Depression Glass Association
119 Wexford Rd.
Brampton, Ontario L6Z 2T5 Canada
Web site: http://www.CDGA.com

Fenton Art Glass Collectors of America, Inc.
P.O. Box 384
Williamstown, WV 26187

Fire-King Collectors Club
1406 E. 14th St.
Des Moines, IA 50316

Fostoria Glass Association
109 N. Main St.
Fostoria, OH 44930

Fostoria Glass Collectors, Inc.
P.O. Box 1625
Orange, CA 92856

Fostoria Glass Society of America, Inc.
P.O. Box 826
Moundsville, WV 26041
Web site: http://home/gte.net/bartholf.fostoria.html

Heisey Collectors of America, Inc.
169 N. Church St.
Newark, OH 43055

National American Glass Company
P.O. Box 8489
Silver Spring, MD 20907

National Cambridge Collectors Inc.
P.O. Box 416
Cambridge, OH 43725

National Candlewick Collectors Club
17609 Falling Water Rd.
Strongsville, OH 44136

National Capital Heisey Collectors
P.O. Box 23
Clinton, MD 20735

National Depression Glass Association
P.O. Box 8264
Wichita, KS 67208-0264

National Duncan Glass Society
P.O. Box 965
Washington, PA 15301

National Fenton Glass Society
P.O. Box 4008
Marietta, OH 45750

National Imperial Glass Collectors Society
P.O. Box 534
Bellaire, OH 43906

National Milk Glass Collectors Society
4600 Kemble
Fort Worth, TX 76103

National Westmoreland Glass Collectors Club
P.O. Box 100
Grapeville, PA 15634

Old Morgantown Glass Collectors Guild Inc.
P.O. Box 894
Morgantown, WV 26507-0894

Paden City Glass Collectors Guild
42 Aldine Rd.
Parsippany, NJ 07054

Tiffin Glass Collectors' Club
P.O. Box 554
Tiffin, OH 44883

Westmoreland Glass Society, Inc.
2712 Glenwood
Independence, MO 64052

Regional

There are many regional clubs where people gather to discuss Depression-era glassware. Check with the National Depression Glass Association for a club in your region if none are listed below:

Arizona Depression Glass Club
2242 E. Campbell
Phoenix, AZ 85016

Big "D" Pression Glass Club
10 Windling Creek Trail
Garland, TX 75043

Black Hills Depression Glass Club
1310 Milwaukee
Rapid City, SD 57701

Buckeye Dee Geer's
2501 Campbell St.
Sandusky, OH 44870

Cambridge Collectors of North Texas
PO Box 180068
Arlington, TX 76096

Carolina Depression Glass Club
P.O. Box 128
Easley, SC 29640

Central Florida Depression Era Glass Club
P.O. Box 948042
Maitland, FL 32794-8042

Central Florida GLASSaholics
P.O. Box 2319
Lakeland, FL 33806

Central Jersey Depression Glass Club
181 Riviera Dr.
Brick Town, NJ 08723

Charter Oak Depression Glass Club
P.O. Box 604
Chester, CT 06412

Chicagoland's Depression Era Glass Club/
20-30-40 Glass Society of Illinois
P.O. Box 856
LaGrange, IL 60525
www.20-30-40society.org

Cigar City Depression Glass Club
P.O. Box 17322
Tampa, FL 33612

Clearwater Depression Glass Club
10038 62nd Terrace North
St. Petersburg, FL 33708

CSRA D. G. Club
1129 Magnolia Ave.
Augusta, GA 30904

Crescent City Depression Glass Club
P.O. Box 55981
Metairie, LA 70055

Depression Era Glass Society of Wisconsin
3935 E. Somers Avenue
Cudahy, WI 53110

Depression Glass Club of Greater Rochester
PO Box 0362
Rochester, NY 14610-0362
http://dgcrochester.org

Depression Glass Club of North East Florida
2604 Jolly Rd.
Jacksonville, FL 33207

Evergreen Depression Era Collectors
312 Golden Gate
Fircrest, WA 98466

Garden State Depression Glass Club
93 Idlewild Ln.
Matawan, NJ 07747

Gateway Depressioners Glass Club of Greater St. Louis
2040 Flight Dr.
Florissant, MO 63031-2216

Great Lakes Depression Glass Club
6363 Livernois
Troy, MI 48098

Greater San Diego Depression Glass Club
P.O. Box 3573
San Diego, CA 92103-3573

Greater Tulsa Depression Era Glass Club
P.O. Box 470763
Tulsa, OK 74147-0763

Green River Depression Era Glass Club
2208 S 223rd
Des Moines, WA 98198

Hazelnut Depression Glass Club
129 Southcliff Dr.
Findlay, OH 45840

Heart of America Glass Collectors
14404 E. 36th Terrace
Independence, MO 64055

Houston Glass Club
P.O. Box 1254
Rosenberg, TX 77471-1254

Hudson Valley Depression Club
Route 52
Walden, NY 12586

Kansas City Depression Glass Club
12950 East 51st Terrace
Independence, MO 64055

Illinois Valley Depression Glass Club
RR 1, Box 52
Rushville, IL 62681

Iowa Depression Glass Association
jeff_wdms@earthlink.net

Land of Sunshine Depression Glass Club
P.O. Box 560275
Orlando, FL 32856-0275

Lincoln Land Depression Era Glass & Pottery Club
21 Foresters Ln.
Springfield, IL 62704

Long Island Depression Glass Society
P.O. Box 148
West Sayville, NY 11796

Low Country Depression Glass Club
209 Trestle Wood Dr.
Summersville, SC 29483

Michigan Depression Glass Society
Livonia Senior Center
Livonia, MI 48154
www.michigandepressionglass.com

Montclair Depression Glass Club
1254 Karesh Ave.
Pomona, CA 91767

Mountain Laurel Depression Glass Club
942 Main St.
Hartford, CT 06103

North Jersey Dee Geer's
P.O. Box 741
Oradell, NJ 07649

Northeast Florida Depression Glass Club
P.O. Box 338
Whitehouse, FL 32220

Nutmeg Depression Glass Club
230 Hillside Ave.
Naugatuck, CT 06770

Old Dominion Depression Glass Club
8415 W. Rugby Rd.
Manassas, VA 22111

Pacific Northwest Fenton Association
P.O. Box 881
Tillamook, OR 97141

Peach State Depression Glass Club
2051 Lower Roswell Rd.
Marietta, GA 30066

Permian Basin Depression Glass Club
1412 Alamosa St.
Odessa, TX 79763

Pikes Peak Depression Glass Club
2029 Devon
Colorado Springs, CO 80909

Portland's Rain of Glass, Inc.
P.O. Box 819
Portland, OR 97207-0819

Sandlapper Depression Glass Club
503 Leyswood Dr.
Greenville, SC 29615

South Bay Depression Glass Society
P.O. Box 7400
Torrance, CA 90504-7400

South Florida Depression Glass Club
P.O. Box 845
Boca Raton, FL 33429

Southern Illinois Diamond H Seekers
1203 N. Yale
O'Fallon, IL 62269

Spokane Falls Depression Glass Etc.
P.O. Box 113
Veradale, WA 99037

Three Rivers Depression Era Glass Society
3275 Sylvan Rd.
Bethel Park, PA 15102

Top of Texas Depression Era Glass Club
42149 1st St.
Lubbock, TX 79424

Tri-State Depression Era Glass Club
RD #6, Box 560D
Washington, PA 15301

Western North Carolina
P.O. Box 116
Mars Hill, NC 28743

Western Reserve Depression Glass Club
8669 Courtland Dr.
Strongsville, OH 44136

Internet Sites

The following Internet Web sites offer information about Depression-era glassware in the form of online articles, references, chats, etc. There are hundreds of Web sites to purchase Depression-era glassware as well as numerous e-auctions.

Dictionary of Glass Marks
> http://www.heartland-discoveries.com

Fire-King.Net
> http://www.fireking.net

Just Glass
> http://www.justglass.com
> P.O. Box 20146
> Cincinnati, OH 45220

Mega Show
> http://www.glassshow.com

PATTERNS BY MANUFACTURER

Anchor Hocking Glass Co.

- ❦ Early American Prescut (see page 172)
- ❦ Forest Green (see page 214)
- ❦ Manhattan (see page 271)
- ❦ Moonstone (see page 295)
- ❦ Oyster & Pearl (see page 327)
- ❦ Royal Ruby (see page 387).
- ❦ Wexford (see page 460)

Note:
This chapter lists
only patterns
included in
this book.

Forest Green by Anchor Hocking Glass Co.

Victory by Diamond Glass-Ware Co.

Belmont Tumbler Co.

❦ Rose Cameo (see page 373)

Dell Glass Co.

❦ Tulip (see page 441)

Diamond Glass-Ware Co.

❦ Victory (see page 452)

Duncan & Miller Glass Co.

❦ Sandwich (Line #41) (see page 396)

Colonial Fluted by Federal Glass Co.

Federal Glass Co.

- ❦ Colonial Fluted (Rope) (see page 126)
- ❦ Columbia (see page 128)
- ❦ Diana (see page 160)
- ❦ Georgian (see page 222)
- ❦ Heritage (see page 227)
- ❦ Madrid (see page 266)
- ❦ Mayfair (see page 275)
- ❦ Normandie (Bouquet and Lattice) (see page 313)
- ❦ Park Avenue (see page 330)
- ❦ Parrot (Sylvan) (see page 332)

❦ Patrician (Spoke) (see page 334)

❦ Pioneer (see page 347)

❦ Raindrops (Optic Design) (see page 364)

❦ Rosemary (Dutch Rose) (see page 375)

❦ Sharon (Cabbage Rose) (see page 409)

❦ Star (see page 419)

❦ Thumbprint (see page 439)

❦ Yorktown (see page 468)

Star by Federal Glass Co.

Fenton Art Glass

- ❦ Lincoln Inn (see page 260)

Fostoria Glass Co.

- ❦ Fairfax (No. 2375) (see page 187)

Hazel Atlas Glass Co.

- ❦ Aurora (see page 66)
- ❦ Cloverleaf (see page 115)
- ❦ Colonial Block (see page 124)
- ❦ Florentine No. 1 (Old Florentine, Poppy No. 1) (see page 203)
- ❦ Florentine No. 2 (Poppy No. 2) (see page 206)

Aurora by Hazel Atlas Glass Co.

Fruits by Hazel Atlas Glass Co.

Hazel Ware, Continental Can

Hocking Glass Co.

- ❦ Block Optic (Block) (see page 77)
- ❦ Bubble (Bullseye Provincial) (see page 84)
- ❦ Cameo (Ballerina, Dancing Girl) (see page 91)
- ❦ Circle (see page 112)
- ❦ Colonial (Knife and Fork) (see page 118)
- ❦ Coronation (Banded Fine Rib, Saxon) (see page 131)
- ❦ Fortune (see page 218)
- ❦ Hobnail (see page 232)
- ❦ Lake Como (see page 255)
- ❦ Mayfair (see page 277)
- ❦ Miss America (see page 286)
- ❦ Old Café (see page 315)
- ❦ Old Colony (Lace Edge, Open Lace) (see page 319)

Miss America by Hocking Glass Co.

Diamond Quilted by Imperial Glass Co.

Imperial Glass Co.

Indiana Glass Co.

- ❦ Avocado (see page 68)
- ❦ Christmas Candy (No. 624) (see page 110)
- ❦ Cracked Ice (see page 133)
- ❦ Daisy (No. 620) (see page 144)
- ❦ Horseshoe (No. 612) (see page 241)
- ❦ Indiana Custard (Flower and Leaf Band) (see page 244)
- ❦ Lorain (see page 263)
- ❦ Old English (Threading) (see page 322)
- ❦ Pineapple & Floral (No. 618) (see page 344)
- ❦ Pretzel (No. 622) (see page 349)
- ❦ Tea Room (see page 434)
- ❦ Twiggy (see page 443)
- ❦ Vernon (No. 616) (see page 450)

Tea Room by Indiana Glass Co.

Jeannette Glass Co.

- ❦ Adam (see page 50)
- ❦ Anniversary (see page 62)
- ❦ Cherry Blossom (see page 101)
- ❦ Cube (Cubist) (see page 137)
- ❦ Dewdrop (see page 152)
- ❦ Doric (see page 167)
- ❦ Doric & Pansy (see page 169)
- ❦ Floragold (Lousia) (see page 194)
- ❦ Floral (Poinsettia) (see page 197)
- ❦ Harp (see page 225)
- ❦ Hex Optic (Honeycomb) (see page 229)
- ❦ Holiday (Button and Bows) (see page 234)
- ❦ Homespun (Fine Rib) (see page 238)
- ❦ Iris (Iris and Herrringbone) (see page 246)
- ❦ National (see page 304)
- ❦ Sierra (Pinwheel) (see page 415)
- ❦ Sunburst (Herringbone) (see page 427)
- ❦ Sunflower (see page 429)
- ❦ Swirl (Petal Swirl) (see page 431)
- ❦ Windsor (Windsor Diamond) (see page 464)

Lancaster Glass Co.

L.E. Smith

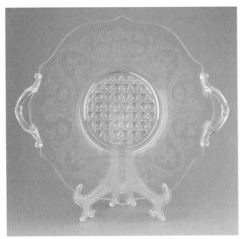

Patrick by Lancaster Glass Co.

Macbeth-Evans Glass Co.

- ❦ American Sweetheart (see page 57)
- ❦ Chinex Classic (see page 108)
- ❦ Cremax (see page 135)
- ❦ Dogwood (Apple Blossom, Wild Rose) (see page 164)
- ❦ Petalware (see page 340)
- ❦ S Pattern (Stippled Rose Band) (see page 393)
- ❦ Thistle (see page 437)

Thistle by Macbeth-Evans Glass Co.

Cupid by Paden City Glass Co.

McKee Glass Co.

❧ Laurel (see page 257)

New Martinsville Glass Co.

❧ Moondrops (see page 290)

Paden City Glass Co.

❧ Cupid (see page 141)

Unknown maker

❧ Bowknot (see page 82)

❧ Round Robin (see page 380)

U.S. Glass Co.

- Aunt Polly (see page 64)
- Cherryberry (see page 106)
- Floral and Diamond Band (see page 207)
- Flower Garden with Butterflies (Butterflies and Roses) (see page 211)
- Primo (Paneled Aster) (see page 352)
- Strawberry (see page 424)
- U.S. Swirl (see page 448)

Westmoreland Glass Co.

- Della Robia (#1058) (see page 148)
- English Hobnail (Line #555) (see page 176)

U.S. Swirl by U.S. Glass Co.

INDEX